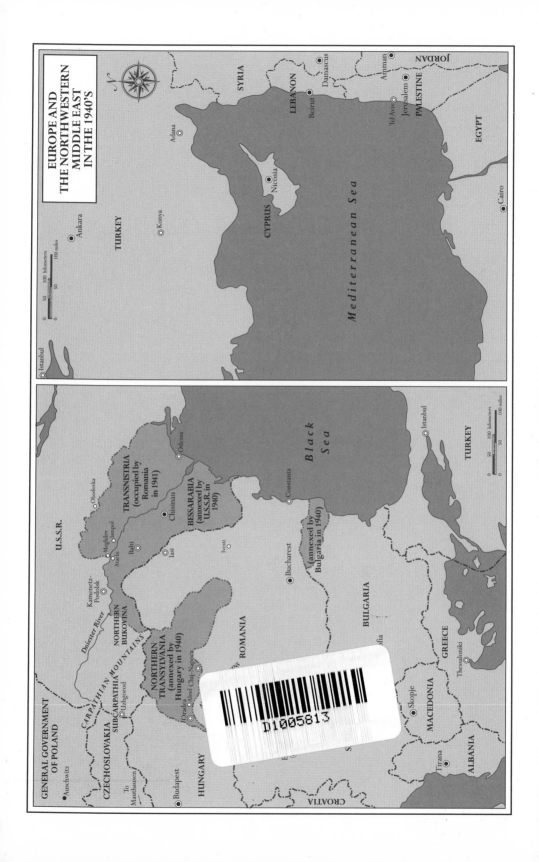

EUROPE AND
THE NORTHWESTERN
MIDDLE EAST
IN THE 1940'S

JOSHUA & ISADORA

JOSHUA & ISADORA

A TRUE TALE OF LOSS AND LOVE IN THE HOLOCAUST

MICHAEL BENANAV

THE LYONS PRESS
GUILFORD, CONNECTICUT

An Imprint of The Globe Pequot Press

The Lyons Press is an imprint of The Globe Pequot Press.

Designed by Sheryl P. Kober

Library of Congress Cataloging-in-Publication Data is available on file.

ISBN 978-1-59921-240-1

Printed in the United States of America

10 9 8 7 6 5 4 3 2 1

For my son, Lucas, and his generation,
who will be too young to know more than a few,
if any, Holocaust survivors.

ONE

On December 3, 1944, a dilapidated 130-foot cargo boat named *Toros* chugged out of the Romanian port of Constanta. The iron plates that usually shielded the ship's wooden hull had been stripped off, for fear they'd attract magnetic mines that bobbed in the Black Sea. Between the seams of the planks newly exposed below the waterline, rags were jammed, staunching a multitude of leaks that threatened to sink the old craft.

The cargo hold—a cavernous space below deck normally used to ferry cattle and sheep across the Bosphorus—had been converted into a floating barracks. Makeshift bunks of bare boards, two rows high, were installed to starboard and port, with an aisle in between. On each side refugees lay three or four across, head to foot, down the length of the hold. Baggage was heaped below in disarray. The lingering odor of livestock was obscured by that of breath and bodies and vomit.

Up above, a phony Red Cross flag flew from the mast. Passengers were deliberately arranged on deck, their heads, arms, and chests wrapped in bandages, completing the ship's disguise as an aid vessel, in hopes of diverting unwanted attention from the Luftwaffe's eager bombers.

The sky was a clear, pale blue, and a brisk, frigid wind swept over the sea-sprayed deck.

The refugees were Jews who, by chance or savvy and usually both, had slipped through the fingers of Nazi Germany's death grip and escaped into Romania, which had fallen behind Soviet lines. Meanwhile, many of their kin, if still alive, were in concentration camps, where more people were being herded into gas chambers in less time than ever before. With the Russians advancing daily from the east and the Allies closing in from the west, the Nazis raced to finish the genocidal task they had set for themselves before the inevitable fall of the Third Reich.

The refugees—homes destroyed, families murdered, memories haunted—were leaving for Palestine, where some hoped to help build a new nation and others to just rebuild their lives. But floating mines and the Luftwaffe weren't the only immediate threats to their dreams. The British, who had controlled the Holy Land since the end of World War I, vigorously enforced a policy curtailing Jewish immigration; in an effort to pacify radical Arab factions in Palestine that had violently protested the growing Jewish presence there. British naval vessels could and did turn back, and even fire upon, ships carrying Holocaust survivors. The boat journey was one last, hazardous hurdle to clear before they could be sure they'd escaped the war with their lives.

But the British, perhaps out of a perverted sense of fair play, had left one loophole in their anti-immigration policy: They agreed to give entry visas into Palestine to a small number of Jews coming from Turkey. So it was for Istanbul that the *Toros* aimed, hoping that bribed Turkish officials would allow the boat to sneak into port.

Among the teeming swarm of a thousand or so passengers was Isadora Rosen. Twenty years old. Skinny and meek. Eyes like dark moons arisen on a face that had forgotten how to smile. She was with her younger brother, Yisrael. Their parents, dead. They were two of the six hundred orphans on board who had somehow emerged from the ghettos and camps of Transnistria—the "Forgotten Cemetery" of the Holocaust, situated in Ukraine—where Romanian Jews had been deported in 1941, in what would prove to be a test run for Hitler's Final Solution. Though less organized, less coldly efficient, conditions in Transnistria were no less cruel than at Auschwitz or any of the Holocaust's icon camps.

There, Isadora had lost most of her family, a few of her toes, and nearly her life.

After Transnistria was liberated by Russian forces, the Romanian government, which worked hand in hand with the Germans to deport the Jews, was forced to readmit those who had survived, but didn't want them to stay. The anti-Semitic regime thus began an odd partnership with Zionist organizations in an effort to send the remnants of European Jewry to Palestine. And the so-called Transnistrian orphans were a priority for both groups.

Disoriented and frightened, Isadora was overwhelmed by the mass of ragged, unruly characters on the overcrowded ship. She had one relative, an aunt, who'd gone to Palestine before the war, but had no idea how to find her. The past loomed behind her like a nightmare, the future before her like a void. With the ship pitching as it motored across the sea, she and her brother went belowdecks, where all but those masquerading as war-wounded were encouraged to ride out the voyage. They squeezed down the aisle between the bunks, looking for a place to lie down.

A seemingly kind, middle-aged man with thinning salt and pepper hair motioned to the confused orphans. "There's some room over here," he said, and pressed closer to the body between himself and the wall. Yisrael climbed up first and settled in next to their new friend. Isadora lay on the outer edge of the board. The hold was filled with a metropolis of sound. Talking and creaking and moaning and retching and yelling and snoring and sniffling. Isadora lay there, still, in the faint amber light from the lamps that hung from the ceiling. Despite the noise, the discomfort, the anxiety, she fell asleep—something that people who've endured great suffering acquire the ability to do, regardless of their surroundings.

She awoke sometime later, feeling the pressure of a hand upon her shoulder. She thought it was Yisrael, who must have shifted in his sleep. But the hand began working its way down her body, groping for the breasts she barely had. Alarmed, she turned and saw an arm draped over her brother's figure, and a questioning smile on the face of the man who'd invited them onto the bunk. She shoved the hand from her body and spastically propelled herself down into the aisle. Pressing her way between those who stood between herself and the door, she stumbled over suitcases and trash to the exit. She had to get out. Her brother, she knew, would be able to fend for himself if he had to.

By this time, night had fallen. The sky was a canopy of stars glistening like silver sequins on a black velvet dress. Isadora didn't notice; she collapsed in a heap on the damp, cold deck. The frigid air stung her cheeks. She covered her face with her hands and wept.

Before long, the beam of a flashlight shone between her fingers. It was held by Joshua Szereny. A Czech citizen, he'd escaped over the Apuseni Mountains from a Jewish slave labor unit in the Hungarian army, while the unit was being marched toward a train bound for Auschwitz. The rest of his family had already been sent there, though he knew nothing of their fate at the time. Through a series of synchronistic events, he'd made his way through Romania and learned of the boat bound for Palestine. Upon making contact with the organizers of the refugee mission, his name was instantly recognized, since his father had been one of Czechoslovakia's most prominent Zionist leaders. Not only was he invited to sail to Istanbul, but thanks to his pedigree, he was also asked to take charge of all aspects of passenger life during the journey, from keeping people fed to maintaining order. It was in this capacity that he stumbled across Isadora, crying on deck, when everyone was supposed to be down below.

"What are you doing up here?" Joshua demanded in Yiddish. Isadora pulled her hands from her tear-streaked face and looked up, uncomprehending. Seeing she was upset and hadn't understood him, Joshua softened his tone and tried again. First in Czech, then German, then Hebrew, and finally, in English. It was all Greek to Isadora. Joshua signaled her to stay put and went to find someone who could translate, assuming she spoke Romanian. He returned with a middle-aged woman, through whom Isadora described the harassment she'd experienced in the bunks. Joshua invited her to come with him to the cabin occupied by the ship's crew. Isadora followed him, but when she saw the room filled with men, she balked and refused to enter. She preferred to ride out the night in the open air. Joshua gathered some blankets, covered her with some of them, then wrapped the others around himself and sat down beside her. They sailed like that, into the dawn, in silence.

In the morning, the translator returned. Joshua asked her to tell Isadora that he had to attend to the ship's business, but if she stayed where she was, he'd come back to check on her. As Joshua began walking away, already besieged by questions from other crew members, the translator shouted for him to return. He paused and retraced his steps until he stood facing Isadora and the translator. The translator turned to Isadora and asked in Romanian, "Do you love him?"

"Love him?!" Isadora replied, flabbergasted. "I hardly know him."

"Well," the translator continued, "do you sympathize with him?"

"Sure," said Isadora. "I can sympathize with him."

After explaining what she'd said, the translator asked Joshua, "And you, do you sympathize with her?" By now, other crew members had gathered around with interest.

"Of course," he said. "I just spent all night freezing with her."

The translator lifted the teacup she was drinking from high into the air and smashed it on the deck. "*Mazel tov!*" she declared. "You're engaged!"

The crew cheered in mock celebration and Joshua waved the translator away with scorn. "You're crazy!" he said. "Get out of here."

As it turned out, she wasn't so crazy after all. ☜══⊱

TWO

Joshua and Isadora are my father's parents. Though I've known them for as long as I've known myself, I've always been struck by, and at first was even a little fearful of, their foreignness. When I was little, I didn't know anyone else like them. They spoke English with thick, Eastern European accents. They pinched my cheeks and called me *boychik*. My grandmother's kitchen smelled nothing like my mother's; though her chicken soup *is* the best in the world, I hated her stuffed cabbage, didn't like the way she cooked chicken, and thought that mandel bread was a poor substitute for real dessert. While plenty of things about them seemed unusual, it was my grandmother's feet that made me truly uncomfortable. A few of her toes were missing, and those that remained were bent and curled and hardly looked human. To a child, they were downright creepy. I was told she'd lost them in the war and understood that something terrible had happened to her. It was something I felt I'd never be able to grasp, since her toes looked like vestiges from a barbaric world so unlike the one I knew that it might've been in another galaxy.

For as long as I can remember knowing anything, I've known how my grandparents met by chance on the *Toros*.

Even as a child, the story struck me as having a mythic quality. Never mind that I didn't know all of the facts back then; the morsels I possessed were plenty for my young mind to chew on. I believed that they alone of all their family members had survived the Holocaust, and imagined them as a modern-day Adam and Eve—the First Man and First Woman of a postwar family whose creation story is set in the anti-Eden of Nazi-occupied Europe. It was as though Hitler had chopped down our family tree at the trunk but, because Joshua and Isadora had survived, it sprouted branches once again. And I was aware of the obvious very early on: that were it not for the Holocaust, my grandparents would never have met, and I would never have been born.

Like most Jewish children, especially the descendants of survivors, I'd been taught that the Holocaust was the zenith of senseless human hatred, the ultimate moral evil, and I believed it. Yet I struggled with condemning it unconditionally, with wishing that it never happened, since my very existence depended upon it. I grappled with trying to reconcile my gratitude for being born with my abhorrence of the circumstances that brought my grandparents together. The workings of the world, I concluded, were not so simple.

In many ways, my recognition of this conundrum at such a young age deeply impacted my perceptions and interpretations of life at a fundamental level. Since my own life—which I judged to be a good thing—was the product of terrible events, I decided that all terrible events were necessary chapters of a larger story which ultimately has a happy ending. This juvenile logic had the surprising effect of turning the Holocaust into evidence that human history, when viewed from a big-picture perspective, travels along an intrinsically benevolent trajectory; that bad things happen in order to produce the better things that follow, even if we can't comprehend in the moment how the world could possibly benefit from whatever tragedy is at hand. Though I no longer believe in such a benign metaphysical reality, my early rationalizations helped infuse me with a still-lingering optimism that breeds hope in dark times, as well as an inclination for making meaning out of the complex contradictions that thrive in the world.

Maybe it seems odd that a child could be so conscious of the dilemmas surrounding his own existence, but for me, there was no way of avoiding it. Every time I had to help someone pronounce my last name (which was just about every time anyone tried to say it), I was reminded. I always knew that my family name, Benanav, was an invention of my grandfather's, and that it had something to do with his escape to Palestine and something to do with the pen name under which his father wrote in Hungary. But it wasn't until I was older—past that age when you yawn at the tales old people try to tell—that I became curious about the details of the origin of my name and the events culminating in its creation.

I sat with my grandparents for many hours over a period of months, asking questions and recording their stories. The more I learned, the more incredible it seemed that they both had found themselves on the deck of the *Toros* at the exact same moment on that cold December night back in 1944. Their lives had been a string of improbable coincidences, luck both good and terrible. Each element of their stories—right down to a mismatched pair of galoshes; a photograph of a Hungarian general; a Romanian Orthodox priest; an SS officer's wife; and maybe, on one occasion, an angel—was crucial to getting them through the war and onto that boat. Had any one of countless small episodes unfolded just a little bit differently, they never would have met and, even if they had both managed to survive, my family would not exist.

With as complete a picture of their early lives as they could give me, I embarked on a trip to Eastern Europe, feeling like the one major piece of the story I was missing was a sense of the places from which they'd come, where they and their families had suffered, and through which they'd made their escapes.

THREE

Her earliest memory:

The sky was a ragged gray quilt with clouds spilling down like dirty cotton from torn seams. The rain had stopped, but the dirt road that ran through the center of the village was still sloppy with muddy water pooled in wheel ruts, hoof marks, and shoe prints. Maybe it was morning, maybe it was afternoon. Isadora, four years old, stood in the small courtyard in front of her house, looking across the street. She knew that the man who lived there, the pharmacist, always had candy, and always gave her a piece or two when she went over to play with his children. She also knew she was supposed to stay in the yard. But her sweet tooth had a will of its own.

She'd been born in the humble white house behind her, there in the village of Ivesti. It was a small, rural place, where peasants grew corn and sunflowers and hauled in their harvests in horse-drawn carts that looked like huge wooden troughs. Cows browsed on the floodplain by the River Siret; turkeys and sheep ranged freely through the town. Houses and courtyards were enclosed by fences draped with morning glories, grapevines, and laundry. Round wells, shared by neighbors, sat beside the streets. There was a bakery and a few shops, but most things were bought and sold at the outdoor bazaar.

Gypsies, whose caravans were parked in a field on the far side of the railroad tracks, went from door to door, selling firewood and inquiring if anyone had any cooking pots that needed repair. Isadora had always been intrigued by their vibrant dress, their music, their *otherness*, and once, she claims, when she was playing near the tracks, she was nearly lured to their camps by an exotic woman who mesmerized her with colorful glass beads. As she began walking away with the Gypsy, she was rescued by a neighbor who took her firmly by the hand and marched her home—though I wonder if it truly happened that way, or if she unconsciously stitched herself into a version of the cautionary tales she'd heard so many times about Gypsies stealing children.

Normally, however, she stayed in the courtyard in front of her house, playing in the garden, as on that gray day when she was possessed by a craving for candy. She could just run over, knock on the pharmacist's door, get a piece or two, and come right back. The longer she stood there, looking through the fence, the better it sounded. In a blue cotton dress that hung just below her knees, with leather boots on her little feet, Isadora reached up, opened the gate, and stepped into the street. She started running, making a beeline for her prize, breaking the cardinal rule impressed upon all children ever since roads were invented— she forgot to look both ways before crossing. In the middle of the street, she slipped in the mud. She landed on her stomach in a puddle, arms splayed before her. As she tried to get up, she noticed the horses for the first time. They were big and black and thundering down the road, hitched to a wagon and heading straight for her. Flecks of mud flew from their hooves. The bells on their tack jangled furiously. They were almost on top of her. She had no time to get out of their way. And the driver didn't see her until it was too late.

Instinctively, she curled into a terrified ball. She felt the pounding of feet inches from her ears, and an instant later heard the high-pitched creaking as the wagon's wheels rolled past on either side of her head. The pharmacist, who had seen her through his window, raced out and picked her up. The driver, who'd pulled his horses to a halt, ran over, fearing the worst. Isadora was crying, filthy, and badly scared, but had escaped unscathed. The men shook their heads in wonder and gently carried her back home.

Isadora's family had lived in Ivesti for generations. One of her great-grandfathers had been a rabbi to the few Jews who lived peaceably among the Gentiles. Her maternal grandfather was a grain merchant who ran a small but profitable business buying and selling corn. When he died, a few years before Isadora was born, Isadora's mother, Anna, was called back from Paris, where she'd been sent to study French. She had a simple, natural beauty, with thoughtful dark eyes and lips that always seemed on the verge of smiling. Her hair was ink black, styled like that of the girl in the Coca-Cola ads from the 1920s.

As things were done in those days, Anna, who was seventeen, was quickly married off to her first cousin, Carol, who was ten years older, in the hope that he'd take over the grain business. But Carol was a lawyer who worked for a firm in the city of Iasi (pronounced *Yash*), 120 miles to the north, and he refused to abandon his profession. He tried for a time to wear both hats, but he only had one head and it wasn't filled with much business sense to begin with. The grain enterprise soon failed.

Isadora was born two years after Carol and Anna married. Anna quit her job teaching French at a local school to stay home with her daughter; eighteen months later, she had a son, Yisrael, whom everyone called Tee-Tee (short for *petit*).

Isadora's early childhood was a sheltered one. Her days were spent in the garden, playing with dirt and flowers and bugs, or in the kitchen, with her mother and grandmother, while they cooked over the wood-fired clay oven in the soft glow of oil lamps. Sometimes she would sit on the adobe floor, scribbling on sheets of paper with a dead coal given to her from the ash bin, blackening her little hands. Her grandmother would sing Romanian folk songs to her, and her mother taught her "Frère Jacques." Despite being the great-granddaughter of a rabbi, none of the adults in her life spoke Yiddish or Hebrew, except for a few basic prayers. Her family observed the Jewish holidays and Shabbat, though they rarely visited Ivesti's small synagogue and could hardly have been called religious.

Even though Yisrael was younger, because he was a boy, he was allowed more freedom to explore the streets of Ivesti by himself or with his gang of friends. Isa wasn't too unhappy with the smallness of her world, though she sometimes wished that she could go out like her brother, look for coins that people had dropped, and lay them on the railway tracks to see them flattened by passing trains. The thing she liked best about the trains and the tracks was that, every Friday, shortly before sunset, they brought her father home after he'd been away all week, working in Iasi, which was too far for a daily commute.

Carol arrived in a three-piece suit—wool in winter, white cotton in summer—with a perfectly folded handkerchief in his breast pocket regardless of the season. Often, he wore a bow tie, and, when in his professional persona, he walked with a cane, though he didn't need one yet. His face and its features were large—a broad mouth, almond-shaped eyes that bulged slightly from their sockets, thick brows that arched high over tired eyelids. His skin was smooth and fair, his light brown hair parted from the far left side of his head.

Anna would be busy inside preparing the Shabbos dinner when Carol swung open the gate and walked across the small yard to their front door. Usually, before he made it there, Isadora had already flung herself at him. He'd pick her up with one arm and enter the house, her small arms clasped around his neck. Like just about any kid whose father's been away, the initial thrill of seeing him was quickly followed by shouts of "What'd you get me? What'd you get me?" For Isa knew that her dad always returned from his week away with small gifts for her and Yisrael. Sometimes Turkish Delight, once a doll as tall as she was.

If it seems like an idyllic family life, despite the fact that Carol was away more than he was home, well, that's the way my grandmother remembers it. Even if you don't believe it, let her have it. She wouldn't have it for long and, looking back over her life, she'd only have it again for brief interludes.

She first noticed something was different on one of those Friday nights. Her father stopped carrying his usual wooden cane and used a longer, white one instead. Soon, he had to be led home from the train station by a friend, and Anna restrained Isa from leaping into her daddy's arms once he got to the house. But she didn't make much of it. After all, she was only five, and no one told her what was going on. When he didn't come home at all one Friday, she was disappointed, but figured he'd had to stay in Iasi to work. Carol, however, had gone into the hospital, and Isadora never saw him again. He died quickly, and probably painfully, from diabetes, or maybe it was cancer, she isn't absolutely sure.

On the day of the funeral, Isadora and Yisrael stayed home with their grandmother, Adela. They saw the procession pass by the house, with a horse-drawn cart carrying a plain wooden coffin. Anna was following, weeping, supported by her brothers and sisters. Isadora didn't know what a funeral was, or what *dead* meant. She still expected to see her father again, as soon as he could return from Iasi.

"Why is Mommy crying?" she asked her grandmother.

"She's very sad," her grandmother replied. It was the only explanation that mattered. ❦

FOUR

Joshua Szereny awoke in the living room of his family's house, on the red cloth sofa where he always slept. It was just before dawn. The fire in the ceramic stove had burned down to coals, leaving the room dark and chilly, but Joshua's nightclothes were soaked with sweat. He'd been a little under the weather for a couple of days with what had seemed like a common winter cold, but now he felt like a knife had been plunged through his ear and into his brain. He held his hands to his head and yelled for his mother. Within seconds, she was at his side. The golden flame of an oil lamp flickered in each lens of her round, wire-framed spectacles. The strong, almost manly features of her normally stern face, glowing in the small pool of light, were drawn with concern. She took his hot cheeks in her hands and asked him what was wrong.

"My ear," Joshua moaned. "My head."

Joshua's mother had never seen him this ill in his ten years of life. She yelled for her husband to get up and fetch the doctor, never mind what time it was. And when Berta ordered, Bela obeyed. He threw a long coat over his pajamas, stuffed his feet into a pair of boots, wrapped a scarf around his neck, and pulled a hat down over his head as the door swung shut behind him.

Berta stoked the fire, put water on for tea, and lit more lamps. Theirs was a simple one-story brick house, like most others in Uzhgorod, with no electricity, telephone, or running water. Fresh water was stored in clay urns kept in the big country kitchen, where a large fireplace gaped like an open mouth in one of the walls. The wooden floor was covered with wool rugs, and the maroon plastered walls were painted with yellow vine-like patterns, creating an effect similar to wallpaper. Three windows looked out past a row of spindly plum trees onto a cobbled street. Berta and Bela slept in the only bedroom with their newborn daughter, Aviva, who was a couple of months old on the night Joshua was so sick. They hoped to move into a bigger place with modern amenities before the winter was over.

Aviva began to fuss, so Berta fetched the baby from the bedroom and paced around the living room, holding her while keeping an eye on Joshua, who tossed on the couch. She spoke soothingly, trying to calm both of her children at once. Her voice, to Joshua, sounded like it was coming through a tunnel. When the doctor arrived, he examined Joshua, poking and prodding, looking in his ears, listening to his heart, taking his temperature. The boy, the doctor said, had a severe middle ear infection and a high fever, and needed to go to the hospital immediately. "Take him to Budapest," he advised. "You'll get the best care there."

Berta bundled Joshua up in his warmest clothes while Bela packed a suitcase for himself and his son. Berta bid them a gentle but tearless good-bye as they left for the station, where they boarded the first train south for the Hungarian capital. In a second-class compartment, Joshua lay across a cushioned bench, wrapped in a plaid blanket, his head on his father's lap. The swaying of the train, the hypnotic clicking and clacking of wheels on rails, lulled him to sleep.

In the muted morning light, the snow-covered Carpathian Mountains, rising over Uzhgorod to the north and east, receded behind them. Before long, the train crossed the frontier into Hungary, a border created just thirteen years earlier, when the Austro-Hungarian Empire dissolved at the end of World War I and the new nation of Czechoslovakia was created from former empire lands. Uzhgorod, once a Hungarian provincial capital, had become a Czech provincial capital, but its citizens maintained strong connections to Budapest—economically, culturally, and emotionally. As the train rattled over the plains, field after frozen field rolled past the window of the Szerenys' compartment. Smoke curled from chimneys poking out of peaked rooftops in the villages that straddled the railway line. Horses hitched to carts halted at the railroad crossings, snorting steam from their nostrils.

Bela was a handsome man, with soft, well-proportioned features and a faint cleft in his chin. His hair was black with a few stray strands of gray and was just beginning to thin. He wore round, tortoiseshell glasses over dark brown eyes, and had a mustache whose edges were precisely aligned with the corners of his mouth. His face naturally conveyed that he was a thoughtful man, while concealing, at first glance, the fiery passions that drove his life. His nine fingers were faintly, permanently stained with printer's ink. He gently stroked his son's hair, grateful that Joshua was able to rest, and tentatively explored the unfamiliar feeling of helplessness he was experiencing.

When they arrived at the hospital, they found that all the beds in the children's ward were full. Fortunately, since Bela had been a highly decorated soldier in the Austro-Hungarian Army during World War I, and dubbed a "Hero of the State," he was entitled to privileged services. Joshua was admitted and placed in a semiprivate room. After being examined by a doctor, Joshua was wheeled into surgery and sedated with ether. The infected bone was removed, but before long, complications set in. The ear continued to bleed on the inside, forming an excruciating hematoma. The doctors had to open the stitches to allow the blood to drain and, until the day he died in 2007, my grandfather had a small hole in the back of his ear. He would never hear clearly from it again.

His recovery was uncertain, this being before the age of antibiotics, and Joshua was kept in the hospital for over a month. If there's an infirmary in Heaven, it couldn't be any whiter than his room was. The walls, the tile floors, the starched bed linens—all implied sterility. As he began to heal, he became friendly with the patient with whom he shared his room, a mustachioed gentleman perhaps fifty years his elder, who was a distinguished Hungarian army general.

With the heads of their beds against opposite walls, the arrangement promoted conversation. Though the man facing Joshua could order thousands into combat with a single phrase, he was less than imposing when lying feebly in a hospital gown, and Joshua never felt overawed. Always a great talker, the boy with smooth, full cheeks, a wide toothy smile, and gleaming brown eyes proved more entertaining for the general than a television would have been. He described his favorite movies, recounting various episodes of *Tarzan*, scene by vine-swinging scene. He told tale after tale from the Old Testament, relating with particular enthusiasm the story of Judah Maccabee and his brothers—which was his favorite—giving the old warrior what amounted to a crash course in Jewish biblical history.

When the general suggested that Joshua might one day join the army and himself fight like the Maccabees, the boy dismissed the idea with his characteristic candor; what he really wanted to be when he grew up was a veterinarian, which his father had told him would be a useful profession once the family moved to Palestine, since the farmers there would need doctors for their livestock. Because he'd been born in a well-integrated city that was a liberal haven for Jews,

Joshua had had no personal experience of anti-Semitism and thus felt no caution about revealing his religious background to a total stranger. The general had nothing against Jews, knowing firsthand that they'd been loyal and courageous soldiers, and he enjoyed the diversions that his young companion provided. Even as a boy, Joshua knew how to tell a good story.

Bela stayed in Budapest for the duration of his son's recovery, taking the opportunity to meet with business and political contacts, and visiting Joshua for hours each day. Initially, Bela was more self-conscious around the general than his son was, since vestiges of the reverence that Hungarian soldiers felt for their commanders lingered in his heart. After becoming familiar with each other, the general asked Bela how it was that he, as a Jew, had a Hungarian surname, and what he'd done to become a war hero; the stories, as the general suspected, were related.

"As you know," Bela explained, settling into a chair, almost but not quite feeling like an equal, "before the 1850s, Jews in Hungary didn't have permanent last names. We simply went by 'son of' whatever our father's first name happened to be. When the decree was issued, instructing us to take fixed surnames, we were forbidden from adopting Hungarian names, since the government wanted to be able to tell at a glance who was Jewish and who wasn't. My family was assigned the name *Szrulovits*—Russian for 'Son of Israel.'

"As a young man, not long out of high school, I had a brief flirtation with socialism, which at the time offered me an outlet to express a deeply felt—though not very well thought-out— sense of idealism. Since I loved to write, I became a stringer for the Viennese newspaper, *Arbeiterzeitung*, covering events in northeastern Hungary. Jews were discouraged from writing for the press, and my last name was a dead giveaway, so I took the pen name 'Bela Szereny,' which struck me as a mildly amusing way of signing my articles 'Anonymous.' " (*Szereny* is Hungarian for "humble.")

"Then, during the Great War," Bela continued, "I was inducted as a private and assigned to a telegraph unit stationed on the front in Galicia." (This was an area formerly ruled by Austro-Hungary, which spans modern-day eastern Poland and western Ukraine.) "As you recall, things went badly for us there in the fall of 1914. By the end of the year, the Russians controlled most of the province, and our greatest ally proved to be the winter, which froze the front lines in place. Though it was cold, it wasn't that bad, really; at least no one for the time being was getting killed. In April of 1915, we received reinforcements."

"Yes," said the general. "Hundreds of thousands of our own troops, plus the entire German Eleventh Army."

Bela nodded. "A massive offensive was in the works, and we hoped to surprise the Russians with overwhelming force."

"The Gorlice-Tarnow," the general interjected, nodding.

"In early May, I was given orders to lead a small team into the no-man's-land between the front lines, and lay telegraph cables ahead of our assault, which would allow the troops to stay in perpetual contact with headquarters as they advanced. Laden with wires and tools, we snuck along the dirt roads, scrambling up telephone poles and hijacking them to our purposes. We carried pistols and rifles, but had no backup and no covering fire. We were completely on our own. The further we could penetrate, the more successful our mission would be, so we crept within earshot of the Russian forces, hoping our speed and stealth would be all the camouflage we'd need.

"It wasn't. I was up atop a pole, rigging our telegraph line, when I was spotted by a small group of Russians on patrol. Before I saw them, they took aim and fired. I was as exposed as an elephant in an open field, and thank God there were no snipers among them, or I'd surely be dead. Only one of their bullets found me, hitting me in the hand and passing clean through one of my fingers. Blood shot out like a geyser. My buddies, who'd fled into the woods, shot back, giving me just enough time to dive into the forest and out of sight before the Russians let loose a fresh volley. We were outnumbered and outgunned, and dangerously close to the Russian camp. The Russians gave chase, but only for a few harrowing minutes of tree-to-tree combat before they turned back. What's funny is that I still remember the smell, an aroma of gunpowder and pine, and I remember thinking at the time how odd it was to even notice such a thing in the midst of battle—it seized my attention the way the full moon, suddenly appearing over a distant mountain ridge, jolts one out of oneself, momentarily overwhelming all of one's senses.

"In the end, I lost a finger, but earned a German Iron Cross. Within days we smashed through the Russian defenses, and before long all of Galicia was back in our hands."

"And it stayed that way," the general added, with satisfaction.

Bela then described a mission a few months later, for which he was awarded a Silver Star, when he slipped into a Russian camp and hid a microphone outside a tent in which top Russian brass met to plan their strategies. Don't ask me exactly how he achieved this, or why the Russians didn't spot the microphone before the Austro-Hungarians were able to obtain valuable intelligence. The specifics of the story have faded to vagaries, bleached by the passage of time, but it's the story I'm told. Even the official records, which prove that Bela did receive these medals, and was promoted to lieutenant, don't offer any details. What I do know is that his decorations entitled him to a land grant after the war, to use the title *Vitez* (meaning "hero") before his name, and to officially change his name to Hungarian—a privilege for which ordinary Jews could apply, but rarely with success.

The general shared with Bela stories of the battles he'd fought and commanded, occasionally dropping his stoic facade and dipping into melancholy reflections on the loss of the war, the dissolution of the empire, and the bruises to Hungarian pride inflicted by the Treaty of Versailles. When he spoke, it was Joshua's turn to listen with rapt attention, absorbing firsthand lessons in modern European history from a man with an intimate connection to it.

On the day the general was discharged, he stood by Joshua's bedside and bid him farewell with a salute, which Joshua, propped up against his pillow, returned. Then the soldier held out a small photograph of himself in his full dress uniform, his chest heavy with medals, which was signed, "To my good friend Joshua Szereny, with love, General Kolbach Karl." Joshua took it with thanks, and propped it up on his bedside table. A week or so later, when he was finally back home in Uzhgorod, Joshua, who was never one to throw anything away, stored it carefully for safekeeping.

FIVE

Joshua's family had lived in the countryside around Uzhgorod for generations, possibly as far back as the days when it was part of the Hungarian kingdom between the eleventh and seventeenth centuries, and certainly during the subsequent rule of the Austrian Habsburgs, which lasted until 1867. With the creation that year of the Austro-Hungarian Empire—a dual monarchy in which Hungary and Austria each governed their own domestic affairs, while united under a single sovereign, the Emperor Franz Joseph— Uzhgorod was returned to Hungarian hands. It remained that way until the end of World War I, when it was ceded to Czechoslovakia. Throughout its history, Uzhgorod has been the capital of a mountainous region laced with fertile valleys, known as Subcarpathia, Subcarpathian Rus, Transcarpathia, and Ruthenia. The names refer to the area's relationship to the mountains and to one of its major ethnic groups, the Rusyns (also known as Ruthenians), the majority of whom were shepherds and peasants who lived in hamlets in the hills.

Joshua's paternal grandfather, Jozsef Szrulovits, was born into a family of peasant farmers in a village about ten miles outside of the city. To escape the poverty for which he seemed destined, Jozsef married a wealthy widow named Pepi Lebovits. She was an older woman with three children, which dimmed her hopes of finding another husband. She'd inherited a vineyard from her first husband, in the nearby town of Csertes, which she and Jozsef quickly sold. With the proceeds, they rented a house on a large piece of property on Uzhgorod's outskirts and built a barn and stables. They bought enough cows to start a profitable dairy and purchased horses and coaches, called *fiakas*, with which Jozsef ran the nineteenth-century version of a taxi company. Bela, their first child, was born in 1892, followed by two daughters, Margaret and Lily.

Jozsef and Pepi were both Jewish, but he was much more religious than she. Her father had been so unobservant that his own brother changed his last name in disgust, saying he didn't want to be associated with someone who broke so many commandments. Jozsef's father, however, took his faith seriously enough that when his daughter became betrothed to a Christian, he tore his clothes and wrote her off as dead, with none of the tortured misgivings expressed by Tevye the dairyman after his daughter, Chava, did the same in Sholom Aleichem's most famous story.

Jozsef's religious background and his quest for enhanced personal prestige fused into a singular desire: to have a rabbi in the family. The task fell to Bela, his only son, by default. Like many Jewish boys in the region, Bela received his elementary education at a *cheder*, where the course of study focused exclusively on religious subjects and the mastery of Hebrew prayers. After his bar mitzvah, he was sent off to a rabbinical seminary in Austria.

One early-spring morning in 1907, when he was fourteen years old, Bela returned home for Passover break after months away at school. Dressed in a long coat and carrying one small suitcase, he got off the train in Uzhgorod and aimed for the row of horses, carriages, and drivers waiting for fares outside the terminal. He scanned the *fiakas*, looking for Jozsef, who always came to pick him up at the station. But Bela didn't see him. After waiting a few minutes, he figured his father must be otherwise occupied and began the couple-mile walk to his family's house without giving it too much thought. The air was brisk but the sun was bright, one of those days that looks like spring but still feels like winter. The steeples and domes that rose from the city's churches gleamed behind him, and the centuries-old castle loomed high above on the hill.

Before long, Bela tasted smoke in the air; had this been autumn, it wouldn't have been unusual, but this was the season for planting fields, not scorching them. Rounding a bend in the dirt road, his home came into view; where the barn and stables should have been, a tidal wave of flames roiled against the sky. Bela dropped his suitcase and ran to help his parents and their neighbors, who scurried around frantically, shouting to one another over the explosive crackle of burning wood and the wailing of animals, trying to douse the inferno with buckets of water. They might as well have been throwing snowballs at the sun. In the end, little was left beside charred timbers, blackened mud bricks, and smoking horse and cow carcasses. The family had lost virtually everything, including the future as they had planned it. It was the worst Passover they could imagine.

Instantly thrust into poverty, Jozsef could hardly afford to feed his children, let alone pay the tuition for Bela's rabbinical training. Instead of returning to Austria, Bela was sent to live with an aunt in Bekeschaba, in southern Hungary, to ease the financial burden on his family. His sisters remained at home. Since Jozsef and Pepi could no longer provide either of the girls with a dowry, their futures looked bleak; the best they could realistically hope for was to marry poor peasants—a nightmarish prospect for their father, who knew the hardships of that kind of life all too well. Jozsef concluded that his daughters' best option was to leave Europe altogether.

The girls had a half sister, Rose, from Pepi's previous marriage, who'd run away to New York years earlier after eloping with an artist whose Bohemian ways Pepi loathed. When Margaret was sixteen, Jozsef secretly wrote to Rose, knowing that Pepi wouldn't deign to beg her renegade daughter for help. Rose replied that she'd gladly take Margaret in, and sent money for her passage to America. By the time the arrangements were made, the momentum of events—along with the growing recognition that the family wasn't going to rise from poverty anytime soon—overcame Pepi's weak protests, and Margaret eagerly left for the States. After a few years of working in New York as a seamstress, Margaret sent for Lily. Both married fine, respectable men, and, most important, were a world away by the time the rest of their family was deported to Auschwitz. The fire, in the end, had proved more providential than catastrophic for them.

The course of Bela's life—as well as, eventually, that of the entire Jewish community of Uzhgorod—would also be altered by the blaze. His aunt Ethel, who thought that the last thing the world needed was another rabbi, talked him out of becoming one. She exposed him to literature, philosophy, and music, and sent him to public school to get a secular education. Bela, who had only undertaken religious studies because his father imposed it upon him, flourished, his young mind soaring nimbly, exultantly, on currents of intellectual freedom unknown to him in the seminary or at home. Upon graduating from high school, Bela moved to the village of Berezna, some sixty miles as a crow flies from Uzhgorod, tucked in a small river valley among the folds of the Carpathians. There, he apprenticed with a lawyer ("Like," my grandfather added as he told me this story, "you remember Lincoln?"), and began writing for *Arbeiterzeitung*.

Bela didn't know that at the time he was writing for the newspaper, it was being closely read by a certain destitute, aspiring painter living in Vienna, who had no affinity for the socialist agenda but was nonetheless impressed by the party's ability to master the hearts and minds of millions; he began an almost scientific study of their propaganda techniques, including reading the paper that he called a "wretched thing" whose "tone was a sort of mental vitriol."

Among the lessons Adolf Hitler absorbed from the socialist political machine was that "no means were too base, provided they could be exploited in the campaign of slander." He observed the effectiveness of waging "a campaign of mental terrorism against [those] who are neither morally nor spiritually equipped to withstand such attacks." He recognized the power of "intimidation in workshops and in factories, in assembly halls and at mass demonstrations," and he saw that employing these tactics "based on an accurate estimation of human frailties must lead to success, with almost mathematical certainty."

While in Berezna, Bela befriended a family of Zionists, who exposed him for the first time to the ideas of Jewish nationalism, and began persuading him of the importance of founding a Jewish homeland. The year was 1912, sixteen years after Theodore Herzl had published *The Jewish State*, in which the essential principles of Zionism were laid out. It was fifteen years after the first Zionist Congress was held in Basel, Switzerland, creating what amounted to a Jewish parliamentary assembly that called for founding a Jewish state in Palestine and strengthening the sense of shared national identity among Diaspora Jews. It was nine years after the brutal Chisinau pogrom prompted calls from around the world to provide Jews with a country of their own; and it was just five years before the British government issued the Balfour Declaration, pledging support for "the establishment in Palestine of a national home for the Jewish people."

Yet in Hungary, at that time, the Zionist movement had but a toehold. It had hardly penetrated into Subcarpathia, where Bela grew up, thanks to the moat of religious orthodoxy that surrounded the province. Most ultra-Orthodox Jews believed it a sin to actively strive for a homeland in Israel, since the Scriptures promise it will be delivered by the hand of God, at His convenience, with the coming of the Messiah. For Jews to reclaim Israel themselves was a total abdication of faith in the biblical prophecies of Messianic redemption, amounting to heresy. Ultra-Orthodox rabbis also attacked Zionist activities aimed at improving conditions for Jews in their Diaspora homelands. Adhering to the reactionary theological principle that "all that is new is biblically prohibited," they railed against the inauguration of Jewish schools in which science, literature, and other secular subjects were taught, denounced the rise of Hebrew as a conversational and not exclusively sacred language, and shunned the adoption of modern styles of dress.

The seat of ultra-Orthodox influence in Subcarpathia was the city of Mukacevo, a mere twenty-five miles from Uzhgorod. Between 1867 and 1879, Mukacevo's chief rabbi, Hayyim Sofer, ordered his followers to avoid contact with any Jews or Jewish organizations that promoted change. "The central principle," he said, "is to distance oneself from the innovators." He went so far as to forbid mourning for Zionists at their funerals. Even so, Mukacevo's Orthodox community forced him from his post for being too progressive. He was replaced by what would become a dynasty of hard-line Hasidic rabbis from the Shapira family, culminating with Hayyim Elazar Shapira, Eastern Europe's most venomous religious adversary to Zionism in the 1920s and '30s, who became a sworn enemy of Bela Szereny.

In the other regions of Hungary, including where Bela went to high school, most Jews were assimilationists, defining themselves as Hungarian, speaking Hungarian, and trying to blend in completely with mainstream Hungarian culture. They pointed to the fact that since 1867, Jews had been full Hungarian citizens and had equal rights under the law. Of course, the assimilationists were well aware of the robust anti-Semitic sentiments of many Hungarian Christians, but felt that their best defense against intolerance was to be more Hungarian rather than more Jewish.

With little welcome for Zionism in Hungary's Jewish communities, Bela was twenty years old before he got his first real taste of it. The friends he made in Berezna discussed with him Herzl's ideas that all Jews everywhere are one people; that their collective problems could only be solved by establishing a Jewish homeland; and that such a goal was in fact attainable. Herzl's message slowly worked its way into Bela's bones. His transformation into a Zionist started with a shift in his perceptions of himself; gradually, he began to identify as a Jew who happened to be Hungarian, rather than a Hungarian who happened to be a Jew.

Two and a half months before Bela's twenty-second birthday, on June 28, 1914, Archduke Franz Ferdinand of Austria—the heir to the empire—was assassinated in Sarajevo by a Serb nationalist. This was the spark that ignited World War I, and by early August, sides were drawn and hostilities begun. Bela was soon impressed into the Austro-Hungarian army and told to report to a draft office. The room was filled with other soldiers-to-be waiting in line to register for service. On the walls hung framed pictures of a uniformed Franz Josef, whose shaggy white muttonchops covered his cheeks and joined together in a mustache, leaving his chin bare. When Bela approached the desk, the officer sitting behind it began to interview him, filling out the first pages of his army records. After coving the basics, such as full name, date of birth, and place of birth, the officer asked Bela to state his nationality.

"Jewish," Bela replied.

"That's no nationality, it's a religion," said the officer. "You can be Hungarian, Czech, German, Slovak, or the like, but 'Jewish' means nothing."

"Then I am nothing," Bela said.

They took him anyway.

Despite the rigors of combat, his heroic escapades, and the loss of a finger, the most transformative of Bela's wartime experiences occurred not on the battlefield, but in the villages in which he was stationed. It was there that he encountered the Jews of Galicia on their own turf for the first time; he had known them before only as impoverished immigrants to Subcarpathia, and by their reputations as *Galicianers*, which was a common slur used to imply that someone was of the lowest class of Jew possible and probably had criminal tendencies. The only insult more cutting was to be called a Gypsy. Witnessing the squalor in which the Jews of Galicia lived and the lack of pride they had in themselves and for their heritage shook Bela profoundly.

From the front, he sent a letter to his best friend, Ignaz Steiger, in which he wrote:

> *The voice of the common people has become for me the same voice as the thunder on Sinai heard by our ancestors. Here on the front I became a Zionist; I find myself thinking only of the honor of our race, and how I can make a difference to our people. I feel that that's the road I have to go and will go. I live here among the Jews of Galicia. When I look at them my heart aches.*

At least if they were knowledgeable of their religion . . . but they are not. When I look at them they seem like they are apologizing for being Jewish, for even being alive. Their condition affects me so much that I've decided to help them as much as I can, and every other day I meet with local Jews to talk about what it means to be Jewish, and how they can organize to help themselves. I have enthusiastic attendance, and often at the meetings I teach them Hebrew, including the women. I hope that my being here will help uplift our people.

With the zeal of someone who's been born again, Bela preached the gospel of Zionism to the other Jewish soldier in his unit, a man named Jyula Raif, trying to convert him to the cause. Raif, however, dismissed the notion of a country of Jews as a far-fetched pipe dream. Once, in their barracks, Bela was holding forth on the subject while Raif was writing a letter. In an attempt to get some peace, Raif said, "I'm writing to a cousin who's as crazy a Zionist as you. Maybe you'd like to express yourself to someone who cares?" Since Zionists felt a close sense of brotherhood with each other, Bela took the pen and eagerly added a short note of support to the end of the letter. When Raif heard back from his cousin, whose name was Berta Freiberg, there was a postscript at the bottom for Bela. From then on, every time Raif wrote to Berta, Bela would add a few words, and soon the two Zionists began corresponding independently. Bela kept in frequent touch with Berta, wherever his duty sent him; when paper was unavailable, he'd post letters to her scribbled on tree bark or rags.

Berta had grown up in the Slovakian village of Zabokreky, which had a small Jewish community led by a very liberal rabbi. The rabbi's niece, who happened to live with him, was Berta's best friend. The two girls spent most of their days at the rabbi's house and, since he loved to tell stories and Berta loved to listen to them, she acquired a rich background in Jewish and biblical history. Thanks to the way the rabbi taught, she felt personally linked to the Jewish past, so by the time she was first exposed to Zionism as a teenager, she was ripe to embrace it. What's more, she had many times heard a story that took place years earlier, which conveyed to her the vulnerability of Jews in a Gentile world.

The year was 1848, and Hungarian nationalists had revolted against the Austrian monarchy, fighting for independence from the Habsburgs. A group of Russian mercenaries hired by Austria to help quell the rebellion stopped to eat at the inn owned by Berta's grandparents. When they finished their meal, they accused Berta's grandmother of trying to poison them, though of course no one appeared to be ill. But no matter. They seized Berta's grandmother, hauled her outside, and tied one end of a rope around her neck. The other end they fastened to a horse. Then, they gave the Jews in town one hour to fork over a hefty ransom. If they failed to produce it, the mercenaries would ride off, dragging Berta's grandmother to the next village. She stood there in her noose, calm and digni-fied, the story goes, while her husband raced around in a panic, emptying his own cash box and begging and borrowing whatever he could from other members of the temple's congregation. The price was paid with just minutes to spare, and Berta's grandmother was cut free. Such a thing, Berta thought, could never happen to a Jew in a Jewish country.

In 1919, when the war was over, Bela went to meet his pen pal for the first time. After years of correspondence, they already knew each other well, and Bela wasn't dismayed when Berta proved to be less than a great beauty. He loved and admired her for her values and her intellect, and neither he nor she could imagine a more perfect partner with whom to embark upon a life centered around the great experiment of Zionism. They were married on September 7, 1920, and settled in Uzhgorod.

⸺⸺⸺

Three months earlier, when Hungary finalized its World War I peace deal with the Allies, it had been forced to cede Subcarpathia to Czechoslovakia. Most important to the Jews living in this newly born nation were the explicit provisions for minorities written into the Czech Constitution, giving them equal rights regardless of race or religion. Moreover, Jews were recognized as a "national" minority—not just a religious one—meaning that they could define themselves as being of Jewish ethnicity to census takers if they wished, and form their own political parties. This was a major victory for the Zionists' agenda, legitimizing their political and social activities and enhancing their campaign to persuade Jews themselves that, regardless of where they lived or what language they spoke, they were all of one people.

Upon returning to Uzhgorod with his new wife, Bela took the money he received from Berta's dowry and from the sale of the land granted to him for his war heroism, and bought a printing press. He opened a commercial print shop and, in 1922, founded a weekly Zionist newspaper, called *Zsido Neplap*, or "Jewish People's Journal." As much a pragmatist as an idealist, Bela published *Zsido Neplap* in Hungarian rather than Hebrew, to appeal to the many secular-minded Jews who didn't speak Hebrew well. Usually four to six pages long, the paper featured local and international Jewish news, Zionist editorials, and dispatches from Palestine. Though one Zionist paper had preceded *Zsido Neplap* in Subcarpathia, it had come out of Mukacevo, and Orthodox opposition shut it down within two years. Bela's paper would become the longest-running Jewish publication in Subcarpathia between the world wars, closing only after the annexation of Czechoslovakia by Germany and Hungary in 1938.

In the same year that *Zsido Neplap* was first published, Bela and Berta's first child, my grandfather Joshua, was born. ❦

SIX

Since Uzhgorod is where Joshua's story begins, it was the logical starting point for my trip to the Old Country. I flew into Budapest, then rode by rail to the southwestern corner of Ukraine, where Uzhgorod sits, just a few miles beyond the Hungarian border.

Some Jews travel back to their ancestral homelands searching for facts to fill gaps in their personal histories. Others go in search of the Righteous Gentiles who saved their parents from the Nazis, or to meet long-lost relatives who happened to survive the war. I wasn't looking for anything so concrete. I simply wanted to see, as much as was still possible, the places that my grandparents saw; to walk in the places that they walked; to set their experiences more accurately in my mind, rather than picturing them in an imagined landscape that might've had little resemblance to the places as they actually looked.

I was after a certain sense of completion, in the same way that a Civil War buff might feel more complete after visiting the battlefield at Gettysburg, or a Christian after walking the Via Dolorosa. Stories, both factual and fictional, have a mysterious ability to inspire geographical cravings. Some of us yearn to stand atop Sinai, others to visit the beaches of Normandy, others to travel to Casablanca or ride the Orient Express; it's different for everyone. The impulse that takes us to those places is more than mere curiosity. Rather, it's as though by stepping into the lands that are important features within the terrain of our imaginations, we seek to inhabit places that have previously inhabited us. By doing so, we connect our inner worlds with the outer, and experience a sense of becoming more whole human beings. The places themselves are more affecting than they would be without their mythos, and the stories live more fully in us than they did before we put ourselves in the places where they are said to have occurred.

Of course, the phenomenon of geographical desire can be collective as well as individual. The struggle over the possession of Israel, for instance, has little to do with what the land itself offers, and everything to do with its story, which might be as much fiction as fact.

Before leaving for Europe, I watched a home video shot in Uzhgorod by my grandfather the last time he visited his hometown, in the late 1980s. On the tape, there were few people out on the streets, none of whom were smiling, and even fewer cars, all old Russian sedans, all driving slowly. The place looked lifeless and drab, perfectly matching my mental image of a typical, small Soviet city. It wasn't the kind of destination to which I'd normally be drawn, and without my personal history, I'd have felt little compulsion to go there. My initial impressions upon crossing into Ukraine only reinforced my presumptions about it.

Standing in line, waiting to have my passport stamped at the Ukrainian customs building in the town of Chop, I took in my surroundings. The ceiling was high and in shambles, with many of its square gray panels haphazardly ripped out, as though by a tornado; some dangled like loose teeth, ready to fall at the slamming of a door. The grungy cement floor was studded with petrified chewing gum. Sunlight slipped weakly through dirty windows. People blew cigarette smoke and crushed the butts under their shoes, oblivious to the NO SMOKING signs hanging on the walls. If I were in a movie, I thought, the film would have just switched from color to black-and-white. The reception hall on the far side of passport control was similar to the first, though this one was dominated by a mural that spread the length of the room, depicting big-muscled, strong-jawed proletariat laborers marching proudly, defiantly, into the future, carrying hand tools and rifles over their shoulders.

My hotel in Uzhgorod had all the charm of your average Communist-era office building. Men in suits, carrying briefcases, passed in and out of the entrance. Nameplates etched in Cyrillic were affixed to the doors that lined the narrow, dark hallways. Through those doors that were open, men and women could be seen sitting behind desks, leafing through piles of paperwork or talking on the phone. Following the hotel clerk, I wondered if I was being taken to look at a place to sleep or start a business. The room I was shown was just large enough for a single bed, a small black-and-white television, and an end table. The musty carpet was the color of rotten meat. The mattress was lumpy and thin, but appeared to be bug-free. A door opened onto a cement balcony with incredible views of the parking lot and dumpsters behind the building. A toilet and sink occupied a bathroom about four feet wide by four feet long, with a showerhead sticking out of the wall and a drain in the middle of the floor.

I left my bag and walked the half-mile to the center of town. It was a perfect, sunny September day. After a couple of blocks, I found myself strolling along cobblestone streets lined with shade trees. Stately brick houses, built in Habsburg times, were plastered in faded pastel hues, from peach to yellow to blue, with carved stone lintels over their windows and doors. Elderly couples sat beneath grape-laden arbors in their courtyards, cleaning vegetables grown in their gardens while chickens bobbed at their feet. Sausages hung in storefront windows, with cheeses and bottles of vodka displayed below them. The street was abustle with cars, which shared the road with horses hauling entire peasant families in wooden carts. I had suddenly, surprisingly, reentered a world of color.

I quickly found the old city center, a buzzing, pedestrian-only arcade of boutiques, churches, and sidewalk cafes. Grade-school kids who'd just gotten out for the day gathered in loud clusters, book bags slung over their shoulders or dropped on the ground, eating ice cream cones, shouting and laughing, playing with and taunting one another. Svelte young women in heels and miniskirts, midriffs bared and cell phones tucked beneath the tresses of their dyed hair, strutted down the brick-paved street like it was a fashion runway. Mothers and fathers pushed baby carriages. Dogs were walked without leashes. Musicians played: here a violinist, there an accordionist. Just about everyone, it seemed, was smiling. There were no policemen anywhere in sight, because none were needed

The elegant buildings, all from old Austro-Hungarian days or earlier, looked freshly refurbished. Though at first glance it seemed like this part of the city might've had one of those pseudo-quaint makeovers that some towns adopt to up their charm factor for tourists, there was nothing phony about it. It was the hub of local life, used by the people who lived there like a shopping mall and a park in one. Boys fished and swam in the River Uzh, and men and women filled the canopied beer gardens perched along the water's edge, drinking, talking, and smoking cigarettes.

Each day I spent there, I became more enchanted with not just the place, but its people. I made more acquaintances more quickly than anywhere I can think of in any of my travels. There were the two women who worked for the People's Union, the political party of Ukrainian president Viktor Yushchenko, who invited me to their office to watch moving video footage, set to rock anthems, of the mass protests during the November 2004 Orange Revolution, which overturned fraudulent election results, ushering Yushchenko into office and a new—if short-lived—moment of idealism into Ukrainian politics. My eyes welled with tears at the sight of inspired throngs enduring a frigid vigil for days and nights on end, demanding that each of their votes be properly counted, asserting through their actions that democracy was worth raising a ruckus for.

There was the musician from a local bar band, who ranked among the best bassists I've ever heard; he doubted he'd ever be able to leave his day job as a taxi driver since his chances of making a living playing music in Ukraine were slim at best, but wasn't willing to give up trying. There was the high school girl who saw me petting a street dog and came over to talk; when I told her I was from the United States, she lit up and said in heavily accented English, "I think, in America, the hot dog is very beautiful." There were the chefs in the hotel restaurant who insisted I come into the kitchen and toast with vodka shots to friendship between our countries. There was the real estate agent who invited me to her parents' house so I could watch her mother make real Ukrainian borscht. The city hummed with a delightful vibe that was impossible to resist, pulsing with optimism at the possibilities the future might bring. It seemed, at its essence, very much the way that my grandfather had described the Uzhgorod of his childhood—except, of course, that there were hardly any Jews.

On my last full day there, I met one. It wasn't by chance. My grandfather had given me the man's name and phone number and told me to call him, saying he was the one person who would know how to find the headstone of my great-great-grandfather, Jozsef Szrulovits, in Uzhgorod's old Jewish cemetery. "He has a book," my grandfather said, "with charts of the graves and who's buried in them." I met Iznac Neubauer in front of what used to be the central Jewish synagogue. Smack in the city's historic heart, it's a stately Moorish-style structure, built of red stone and ochre brick, with three fluted arches for an entrance. It's now Uzhgorod's Philharmonic Hall, since there are hardly enough Jews left in town to make a minyan, let alone fill a temple.

Neubauer spoke neither English nor French, and I didn't speak Ukrainian, Russian, German, or Yiddish. I quickly found that the hotel receptionist, who'd phoned Neubauer for me, hadn't explained why, exactly, I'd wanted to meet him. At first, he thought I wanted to get inside the old synagogue, which is generally off-limits to sightseers. Any effort to verbally explain my purpose to him was useless, so I pulled out my notebook, drew a picture of a gravestone with a Star of David on it and a stick-figure corpse with Xs for eyes lying beneath it, then wrote the name of my great-great-grandfather. Once he understood, he motioned for me to follow him, and we set off down the street.

My guide looked to be in his eighties. His gait was slow and stilted, and his gaunt, creased cheeks were covered with white stubble. He wore gray slacks, a brown-and-white-plaid, short-sleeved shirt, and a white baseball cap. A bluish-gray number—A-3466—was tattooed on his frail left forearm. When we reached a street on the edge of the pedestrian plaza, Neubauer hailed a cab and we got in. After about ten minutes, it pulled to a stop on a narrow dirt road behind a series of apartment buildings that resembled public housing projects. On the right side of the road was a row of shipping containers inhabited by Gypsies, whose laundry was hanging on lines strung along the corrugated walls of their makeshift homes. On the left was a black, cast-iron fence, maybe seven feet high, enclosing an unruly field of about three acres, from which rose stone monuments of varying size and shape. Neubauer took a key from his pocket and opened the cemetery gate.

The place was haunted by neglect. Many of the tombstones were broken; others leaned at angles so precarious that they seemed to violate the laws of physics by refusing to topple over. The grounds were wildly overgrown, giving the impression that decades had passed since they were last tended by a gardener. Bottles and bags of garbage had been dumped over the back fence, providing the finishing touches to the ambiance of ruin. Neubauer, it turned out, didn't have a book showing who was buried where, but he conveyed to me that he thought he remembered the general location of my great-great-grandfather's grave. I followed him along a faint path until he paused and began inspecting each headstone closely. Many of the inscriptions were so eroded that they were impossible to read, so Neubauer clutched a handful of green leaves and rubbed the stones with them, hoping to make the carved Hebrew and Hungarian letters stand out. At the rate he was going, the search would take days, so I left him to look on my own.

Wading through tall grasses, pricker bushes, and wild strawberries, I examined the weathered monoliths one by one; it was an experience similar to leafing through a large book, scanning its pages for one particular sentence you recalled reading in it years earlier, not sure if it was near the beginning, middle, or end. Two hours later, I was ready to give up. I'd talked myself into half-believing that finding the grave wasn't all that important anyway. Maybe, I thought, there was another cemetery and we'd gone to the wrong one. And if this was the right place, well, the stone had simply eluded us. I walked back to Neubauer to tell him the time had come to quit, when I spotted it by chance, covered in ivy and obscured by bushes that surrounded it: a tilted gray slab that said JOZSEF SZRULOVITS, and a lot of other things in Hebrew. I shouted to Neubauer and waved him over to me. On impulse, I pulled the ivy off the stone and cleared the bushes around it with my knife. Though I felt innately that this was what was required of me, I also recognized the futility of the act: The plants would surely grow back, and nobody would return anytime soon—if ever again—to remove them. Nonetheless, I would play my role, then leave the plants to play theirs. It seemed fair enough.

There was only one stone, and only one name on it. My great-great-grandfather was buried alone there; his wife, who should have rested beside him, outlived him to be cremated in Poland. I placed a pebble atop the headstone and paused to ponder the fact that a little bit of the seed I grew from lay buried in this ground. The effect of this realization was subtle, just a flutter within at making a faint connection with a person I'd never known, an era long lost, and a place of which I'd recently grown fond. With nothing else to do, I turned to Neubauer and we left.

We walked toward the main road in silence. At last, Neubauer pointed to his tattoo and said, "Auschwitz." No translation needed. He was the only one of his family to make it out alive, he managed to explain, and now he was one of maybe ten Jews who lived in Uzhgorod. Contemplating this, I was struck with sadness and perplexity. Uzhgorod today seems about as far from a Holocaust as any place could be. That mass deportations had occurred there was almost impossible to imagine. If it was anything before the war like it is now, which by my grandfather's accounts it was, it's easy to see how its Jews had been unable to grasp the reality of the fate that, in hindsight, seems so obviously looming. ⌦⟶

SEVEN

In the summer, the river was his playground. He was never happier to jump in it than on a hot Saturday afternoon, after spending all morning dressed in a suit, attending services, his eight- or nine- or ten-year-old mind wandering away from the prayers and out to the shady parks along the banks of the Uzh. For Joshua, the essence of Shabbat, what he looked forward to all week, was what happened in the hours between morning prayers and Havdalah. His attitude, aside from being that of most normal Jewish children, was actively fostered by Bela, who felt that play was as important to the Sabbath as prayer. Despite his prominent role in the religious life of Uzhgorod's Zionist community, Bela was far from devout. He believed that the primary importance of Jewish ritual lay in preserving cultural traditions—not because it would earn favor in the eyes of God, whom, Bela felt, hadn't done much for the Chosen People in a very long time, if He even existed at all.

Aside from fundamental religious differences, the anti-Zionist rhetoric preached by Orthodox rabbis had convinced Bela that Uzhgorod's Zionists needed a place where they could worship freely, in their own way. Relying on his early rabbinical training, he started a liberal congregation, reworked the liturgy, and created his own melodies to be chanted during services, which he led with a friend. Without a temple of their own, the congregation met in the assembly hall of Uzhgorod's secular Hebrew elementary school, which Bela had helped found in 1922. Joshua, in all his childhood, never once set foot into the grand central synagogue with the Moorish arches in front.

Except for the High Holidays, Bela was never one to spend all day at services. When the weather was good, he was just as eager as Joshua to strip off his temple clothes, put on a bathing suit, and head to the river, where he'd round up a group of children with whom he'd play water polo in the shallows of the Uzh, or soccer on the grassy shoreline. Berta usually came along, too, and though she rarely joined in the play, being far more staid than her husband, she would watch the games from a blanket under a tree, listening to kids and adults shouting gleefully to each other in Hebrew. That Jews could live openly as Jews, she often thought, with so little discrimination, was something of a miracle, and something she couldn't quite trust.

After giving birth to Joshua on November 18, 1922, Berta, as the story goes, said, "That was enough for the next ten years!" And she stuck to her oath. She raised her son in their simple rented home, with no electricity or running water, bathing him in a metal tub, cooking kosher meals on a woodstove. She spoke to Joshua only in her native German, while Bela spoke to him in Hungarian and Hebrew. While Joshua was growing up, Berta proved an indispens-able ally to Bela in his Zionist activities, strategizing with him and lending unfailing moral support. The cause, as Joshua remembers it, was the sun around which their world revolved at a dizzying pace.

While continuing to publish *Zsido Neplap*, Bela won a seat on Uzhgorod's city council in the late 1920s. He lobbied incessantly for the Jewish Party in national parliamentary elections, but the suc-cess he'd found on a local level couldn't be repeated in province-wide polls; though there were more than enough Jewish voters in

Subcarpathia to deliver a few seats in the Czech Parliament to the Zionists, ultra-Orthodox leaders mobilized against them in force. The powerful Rabbi Shapira of Mukacevo attacked with the zeal of a religious fascist, calling Zionists "the destroyers of Israel . . . snakes and scorpions . . . [who] revile the Torah and the laws and commands of our heavenly Father." Just before one round of national elections, he declared: "It is my duty to proclaim that according to our Holy Law it is forbidden to offer the slightest assistance to the Zionist heretics and freethinkers, much less to vote for their candidate, who is a traitor to our Torah. . . . Every Jew must do his utmost to oppose this danger! Furthermore, every Jew who voices an opinion in favor of the Zionist list for Parliament is sinning gravely by abetting the criminals; of the likes of such our Torah says, 'Cursed be he who does not keep the words of this Law!'" The rabbi's influence effectively split the Jewish vote into impotent fragments.

Battles between Bela and Shapira were frequently fought from the pulpits and in the press. As Bela promoted secular Hebrew education, the rabbi pronounced, "Whoever sends his children to the accursed Hebrew school shall be wiped out and shall not be permitted to live to raise his children. The children will not live to see the next year." (When two children from Mukacevo died during an outbreak of typhus, the rabbi declared that it was their punishment for attending such a school.) Bela parried in editorials published in *Zsido Neplap*, and embarked on a cross-continental fund-raising tour, roaming as far as London and Paris in search of donations for the building of a Hebrew high school. When he persuaded the Rothschilds to contribute, the coup reverberated throughout Uzhgorod's Jewish community, giving Bela the aura of being anointed by royalty and bolstering the legitimacy of the Zionist cause. When the school was completed—just in time to admit the first class of students graduating from the Hebrew elementary school—Bela became its president.

Perhaps the fiercest campaign for which Bela held the banner was the Zionist push to persuade Czech Jews to declare themselves as being of Jewish nationality in the 1930 census. Though all people were entitled to the same rights regardless of their ethnicity, minority groups that composed 20 percent or more of the population in electoral districts of any size were entitled to greater funding for their charter schools, and to have their language included among the official tongues in which government business was conducted in that district. In the first national census, in 1920, most Jews were either too habituated to thinking of themselves as nationals of their former countries or afraid of reprisals for defining themselves as ethnically Jewish.

As the 1930 census neared, Bela and his allies found themselves challenged on two fronts: by both the ultra-Orthodox rabbis, who urged their followers to align with the Czech majority, and the ethnic Hungarians, who knew they needed the loyalty of a block of Jews to keep their numbers over 20 percent. The language issue, which touched passionately held sentiments of national pride, inspired a fiercely fought campaign and yanked Uzhgorod's Jews in three different directions. To the Hungarians, their newfound position as a minority was insult enough; the possibility of seeing their language lose its official status was unthinkably degrading. To the Zionists, the chance of having Hebrew declared an official language served no practical purpose, since Jews functioned perfectly well in Hungarian and were free to speak Hebrew or Yiddish among themselves—but a victory would lend a huge boost to the Jewish national cause. Most Orthodox rabbis, of course, strove to defeat the Zionists, since to them, Hebrew was a sacred tongue to be spoken only in prayer.

When the census results were tallied, Uzhgorod's Zionists had won by a slim but significant margin. Hebrew ousted Hungarian from the ranks of official languages, making the Subcarpathian capital the only town in Europe whose mayor had a Hebrew plaque hanging on his door, and its city hall the only one with a sign in Hebrew request-ing visitors to wipe their feet before entering. All Hungarian signs were taken down. It was a bruising blow to the Hungarian ego, and one that would be remembered later with a vengeance.

⸻

As Europe's Zionist movement matured, it became split by infighting between factions seeking to influence the overall direction of the cause. Broadly speaking, there were three types of Zionists: the Labor Zionists, who asserted that any Jewish state should be founded on the principles of socialism; the religious Zionists (includ-ing some progressive members of the Orthodox community, who were the Zionists most despised by Rabbi Shapira), who insisted that any Jewish state must have a Jewish character and a constitution rooted in rabbinic law; and those Zionists who felt that all types of ideology were secondary to the goal of attaining a Jewish homeland in Palestine, which should be pursued as pragmatically and quickly as possible. Bela fell squarely within this last category. Recognizing that the building of a successful Jewish state would require invest-ment capital in industry and infrastructure, and that few serious investors would be attracted to a socialist scheme, he felt that the aims of the Labor Zionists were counterproductive to the primary goal of "upbuilding" in Palestine.

Bela increasingly found his beliefs aligned with those of the out-spoken Zionist leader, Vladimir Jabotinsky, who was also a secular Jew and a former journalist. He rose to international prominence during World War I by advocating for the creation of a Jewish battal-ion within the British army, to help wrest Palestine from Ottoman control. After being appointed in 1924 to the Zionist Executive—the leadership body of the World Zionist Organization—Jabotinsky soon grew frustrated with the movement's lack of progress. He was baffled by the unwavering faith of top Zionist leaders in promises made by the British, who'd been given administrative authority over Palestine following the war, that the groundwork would be laid for a Jewish homeland there. To Jabotinsky's eyes, the British appeared far more concerned with appeasing the Arabs who opposed Jewish settlement in the Holy Land than with honoring their pledge to the Jews. Thus disillusioned, he left the WZO to form an opposition wing, called the Union of Zionist Revisionists, whose sole mission was facilitating the speedy creation of a Jewish state, including the promotion of large-scale immigration.

By 1927, Bela was converted to the cause. *Zsido Neplap* became a Revisionist organ, and, in 1929, Bela was elected as a Revisionist representative to the Central Committee of the Czech Zionist Territorial Conference, the governing body that set the agenda on virtually every issue related to Zionism in the country.

Whenever Jabotinsky passed near Uzhgorod, he visited Bela at his home. With a few other local Revisionist leaders, they sat around the Szerenys' kitchen table, drinking coffee or beer, formulating strategies. Berta hovered nearby, never too shy to contribute her own ideas; Joshua sat beside his father or played on the floor, sometimes listening to the grown-ups, but usually bored by the conversation. During one of these visits, Jabotinsky, well aware of Bela's intentions to leave for Palestine with his family in the near future, asked Bela what proved to be a fateful favor. Would he please reconsider his plans and agree to remain in Europe for a while? He could be of most use by continuing to publish his paper, educating young Jews, and giving others the support and skills they needed to immigrate, Jabotinsky said. Though it would mean postponing their long-held dream, Bela and Berta saw the truth in Jabotinsky's assessment. They agreed to stay. They would make it to *Eretz Israel* one day, they thought wistfully; it would just be later rather than sooner.

EIGHT

It's interesting to me that when I ask my grandfather about his childhood, he tells me about his father. He has very few stories of his own growing up, about things he did or things that happened to him as a boy. When he describes his life back then, he does so in broad strokes; I have to squeeze details out of him. He assumes, for example, that everyone knows what a house looks like, forgetting that few of us who are alive today have ever seen a house in Uzhgorod, Czechoslovakia, in the 1920s. But that doesn't really matter anyway, he thinks, because such details are inconsequential. One could deduce, based on the way he recalls it, that his childhood was hardly consequential. What matters is his father.

He speaks of his father's work and its context as though he understood everything about them while he was growing up, like he is remembering from personal experience. Yet some things he knows about the historical/political setting of the times he must have learned later; he's stitched them seamlessly into his personal memories of events, making it impossible to tell where his own recollections end and the facts he acquired later begin. The sense I get from it is that as a child, Joshua was raised breathing Zionism, bathing in Zionism, eating Zionism for breakfast. Since it is part of him on an almost cellular level, it seems perfectly natural that he appears to be intimately familiar with the ins and outs of the Zionist movement as a young boy, even if that's not exactly the case.

One result of Joshua's deep immersion in his father's world is that what his father did back then is more vivid to my grandfather than what he himself did. But there's more to it than that. He loves his father deeply, and I have little doubt that Bela's murder in a concentration camp made my grandfather's memories of his father more precious than his memories of himself. ⟐⟨⟩

NINE

Soon after her father died, Isadora, her mother Anna, and her younger brother Yisrael moved into the simple mud-brick house rented by her grandmother, Adela. Inside, white plaster flaked from the walls and wooden floors were scuffed by years of wear. In one of the two bedrooms, Isa shared a mattress with Adela and Yisrael, while Anna and her younger sisters—Isa's aunts, Renee and Shoshana—slept on blankets on the floor. The other room was shared by Isa's uncles, Sami, Vili, and Dutsu, who were teenagers. Though it was often loud with the noise of family, Isadora didn't mind the cramped quarters; a steady current of affection buoyed her and made the world tolerable despite the sudden absence of her father. She was still confused and she was still sad, but she was loved.

With the loss of her husband's income, Anna began teaching French at Ivesti's public school, where the salary was meager. Isa's aunts cleaned houses and clothes for wealthier families, while her uncles hired themselves out as farmhands, planting and picking and driving teams of horses that pulled plows and carts. The money they each earned was turned over to Adela, who managed the household and bought whatever food they could afford.

Breakfast was bread and butter, and coffee cut with chicory; lunch was *mamaliga*, the classic Romanian version of polenta; dinner, on a good night, was a pot of beans boiled with onions. On bad nights, they made do with a few onion slices drizzled with oil. Every so often, Adela would manage to tuck away enough money during the week so she could buy a chicken for Shabbat. From one chicken, she could make so many meals, it seemed like a culinary version of the miracle of the Hanukkah oil.

During the day, while Anna was teaching, Isadora was Adela's little shadow. She handed her grandmother sticks with which to stoke the oven. She trailed her to the well by the street and back, the little girl carrying her own small pail of water, the grandmother hefting a large wooden bucketful, each of them clasping one of Yisrael's hands as he walked between them. While Adela filled the kerosene lamps, Isa held the glass globes, forbidden from touching the fuel herself. She picked squash from the garden, allowing her brother to hold one or two, depositing the rest in the folds of Adela's black skirt, which was gathered in front of her to form a basket. After she started attending school, Isa would do her homework on a rug in front of the stove, to the crackle of the fire and the creak of Adela's rocking chair.

After a few years and many discussions, the family decided to move to Bucharest, where they hoped to prosper, or at least creep out of their poverty. Her uncles took their few pieces of furniture by wagon, while the rest of the family boarded the train for the daylong journey south. They settled into an apartment in a multi-unit, single-story building on Dudesti Street, where the poorest of Bucharest's Jews were concentrated. Isadora was seven years old, give or take a year, making it about 1931. She had never been to the capital before, and the bustle of the city captivated her. Fascinated by the street life just outside the courtyard where

she and Yisrael played, Isadora spent many entertaining hours gazing through the gate, her cheeks pressed between its metal bars.
Vendors trolled the neighborhood, hawking their goods with sing-
song shouts. They pushed carts heavy with peppers and squash and
corn, buckets of milk and yogurt, and, most important, water and
charcoal, since the house had neither electricity nor plumbing.
Isadora's favorite peddler of all was a swarthy, mustachioed man
who'd stroll the street carrying a tray filled with Middle Eastern
sweets, like Dudesti's version of the Good Humor man. When
she saw him, Isa would plead for a coin or two, and sometimes
her softhearted grandmother would give in. Most goods could be
bought on credit, and each vendor kept track of their running tabs
by marking their customers' doorways with chalk. The threshold
of Isa's apartment was perpetually covered with red and white
scribbles.

Anna took a position teaching French at a Catholic school.
Though the pay was better than in Ivesti, the work was more
demanding. She frequently suffered from migraines, and spent
much of the time she was home lying down with slices of potatoes on her forehead and over her eyes, held in place with a moist
towel. Times for the family were tougher than ever, since living
expenses in the city were much higher than back in Ivesti. With the
scraps of cloth Sami and Dutsu brought home from their jobs in a
fabric shop, Adela sewed shirts for Yisrael and blouses for Isadora.
Renee found work as a domestic, and Shoshana was sent off to
live with cousins, then immigrated to Palestine by herself. Adela
was forever doing laundry, since no one in the family had more
than a few pieces of clothing. Dinner, more often than not, was
an onion sandwich on black bread. Yet Adela, who tended to the
children far more than their mother did, buffered them from the
desperation lurking in their home, singing to them as she cooked

and cleaned, conveying, through her gentleness and patience, that everything was all right.

Vili provided the kids with some of their brightest moments; as an usher in a movie theater, he earned little, but was able to let his niece and nephew in for free once they grew a little older. Isadora became enchanted by Shirley Temple, returning time and again to the sanctuary of the cinema to watch the young heroine sing and dance her way through her tribulations, often as an orphan, to her happy endings. Though Isa had no idea what the lyrics meant, she memorized, more or less, the words to "On the Good Ship Lollipop," and other Temple hits, and tried to teach them to her grandmother.

At the public elementary school, Isadora's class was a melting pot of young Jews and Gentiles. At a glance, with her blonde hair and fair skin, Isa could have easily been mistaken for the latter. The only time she felt "different" was when religion—meaning Christianity—was taught, and the teacher asked the Jewish students to leave the classroom and sit in the hall. She made friends easily with other children, regardless of their backgrounds, which didn't matter much to anyone on the playground. A few years later, Isadora's family would be very glad that she'd made one Gentile friend in particular.

The years between 1923 and 1938 have been called "a golden age of human rights in Romania," a country which had long been regarded as Russia's equal as the most anti-Semitic in Europe. In the fifteen years between 1899 and 1914, some 100,000 Jews fled Romania for places less repressive. Most of those who remained lived in dire poverty. At the end of World War I, Romania and its Jews reaped the dividends of the Allied victory. The regions of Transylvania in the west and Bukovina in the north, long ruled by the Austro-Hungarians, were repatriated to Romania, as was Bessarabia, in the east, which had been annexed by the Russians in 1912. In exchange for this generous settlement brokered by the Allied Powers, Romania agreed to grant full citizenship to its minorities, along with equal civil and political rights. These conditions were met in a new constitution, adopted in March 1923.

Things got better for the Jews, as professional and educational opportunities opened up to them. Yet their sudden trajectory toward the Romanian mainstream also triggered an anti-Semitic backlash. Pogroms erupted across the country throughout the 1920s, inspired by the charismatic leaders of ultranationalist political movements, the most prominent of which was the Legion of the Archangel Michael. The Legion was a religio-fascistic movement comprised of, essentially, political terrorists. Over the next decade, employing a strategy that could have been a model for Hamas or Hezbollah, the Legion won support among the peasantry by building churches and schools, funding charities, supplying aid to poor communities, and railing against government corruption. They staged electric political rallies, with members decked out in green shirts chanting chauvinistic slogans, singing patriotic hymns glorifying the Romanian people, and declaring the Jews to be the scourge of the nation. The militant fanatics lynched Jews, threatened Gentiles who would "collaborate" with them, and eliminated political enemies, even assassinating the Romanian prime minister in 1933.

Though there were troubling signs emerging across the sociopolitical landscape, it remained a time of hope and progress. In the Dudesti neighborhood, residents of all backgrounds were more united by their poverty than divided by racial or religious differences, and the civil rights of the Jews were still protected by law. But laws, of course, have no guaranteed lifespan. ⌫⟶

TEN

As the 1930s progressed, Romania descended into political turmoil. An epidemic of corruption blighted every branch of government. The global depression devastated the economy, offering a golden opportunity for the Legion of the Archangel Michael (also known as the Iron Guard) to blame Jewish businessmen for the hardships crippling the country. The Gentile population flocked to the fascists' call to disenfranchise Jews and bar them from a broad spectrum of professions, and the Legion gradually moved from the fringes toward the political mainstream. Once it was swept into top government positions on a surge of popular support, a profusion of anti-Semitic legislation was enacted—even more radical than Germany's Nuremburg Laws. At the same time, international events beyond King Carol's control accelerated the rate at which Romania plummeted into chaos.

Over the summer of 1938, Hitler threatened to invade Czechoslovakia, claiming that the region of Sudetenland, with its large ethnic German population, rightfully belonged to Germany. After months of negotiations, Italy, France, Germany, and Britain signed the Munich Pact on September 29, 1938, which has stood ever since as a symbol of the foolishness of appeasing tyrants. The pact, which permitted Germany to occupy the Sudetenland—a first step in the total dismemberment of Czechoslovakia —set a precedent for rolling back the peace deals that concluded World War I. Hungary soon began clamoring for the Transylvanian territory it had returned to Romania after signing the Treaty of Versailles, and the Soviet Union threatened to retake Bessarabia from Romanian hands.

Any sense of security to which King Carol clung was stripped away in 1939 with the outbreak of World War II, as international borders became as fragile as glass. He felt compelled to tacitly ally himself with Hitler, offering the German army access to oil-rich fields, hoping that the Führer would safeguard Romania's territorial integrity from Hungarian and Russian desires.

On June 26, the Soviet Union gave Romania twenty-four hours to relinquish Bessarabia, along with the region of Northern Bukovina, or face the military consequences. Hitler looked the other way. Fearing that resistance would turn Romania into another Poland, occupied and divided between Germany and the USSR, Carol capitulated. As the Romanian army withdrew from Bessarabia and Northern Bukovina, its troops were harassed by the local peoples they left behind; they were taunted and had garbage thrown at them, and were even assaulted. As ceding the territory had wounded Romanian pride, the army's send-off was taken as a mortal insult. Newspaper articles falsely blamed the attacks on spiteful throngs of Jews eager to embrace their new Communist leaders. Soon, the entire country was whipped up into an anti-Semitic frenzy, and no segment of it more so than the military.

Once over on the Romanian side of the new borders, army units massacred Jews for revenge, in numbers as small as a handful up to hundreds at a time. Even Jewish soldiers were murdered by their Gentile counterparts. Jewish property was seized or destroyed, women raped, children and the elderly shown no mercy. The reprisals cooled off after a few weeks, but the army wouldn't have to wait long for another opportunity to brutalize the Jews—and on a scale that few could have envisioned.

Fearing that taking Bessarabia was only a first step in Stalin's designs on Romanian lands, King Carol officially joined the Axis Powers. Hitler, however, agreed to defend Romania from Russia only if Carol accepted a German-imposed settlement to the dispute with Hungary over Transylvania. Carol, powerless to argue, was forced to give to the Hungarians 40 percent of the region that Romanians considered the heart and soul of their country. Within hours, the Iron Guard had mobilized, flooding the streets of Bucharest with tens of thousands of outraged citizens and seizing state buildings on September 3, 1940. The monarchy teetered on the verge of collapse. Carol ordered the army to fire upon the mobs outside the palace who were clamoring for his abdication, but the generals refused to comply. Only one man, it was agreed, could possibly restore order. General Ion Antonescu was summoned to an emergency meeting with the king.

Known as the "Red Dog," both for the color of his hair and his bloody suppression of a peasant revolt years earlier, Antonescu was an astute military strategist with a reputation for being incorruptible. His intellect was sharp, his ego inflated, and he often referred to himself in the third person. The French general, Victor Pétin, who came to know Antonescu during the 1920s when he served as Romania's military attaché to Paris, described him as having "a well-tried intelligence," while also being "brutal, duplicitous, very vain, [with] a ferocious will to succeed—these are, together with an extreme xenophobia, the striking characteristics of this strange figure." During the 1930s, Antonescu had served short stints as chief of staff of the Romanian army and, later, as defense minister, but he appeared to have no political aspirations for himself, nor deep allegiances to any party.

As the crisis intensified over the first few days of September 1940, Carol and Antonescu met several times. Even had he wanted to, Antonescu could not save Carol's crown. On September 6, the king abdicated in favor of his nineteen-year-old son, Michael, who promptly gave Antonescu unlimited dictatorial powers over the country, turning himself into a figurehead. Carol fled the country, with as much of the Romanian treasury as he could carry.

Antonescu, who took the title of marshal, found himself in an awkward position: Although he was the leader of a nation, he had no political base. While he sympathized with the Iron Guard's anti-Semitic enthusiasm, he scorned it for its lack of discipline and for the wild upheavals it had fomented throughout the country. Yet since the Guard was by far the dominant force on the Romanian street and enjoyed the support of Germany, he had to work with it, and Legionnaires were appointed as top cabinet ministers. Likewise the Guard, as much as it craved total authority, needed Antonescu, since his voice was the one to which the army would respond. Romania, thus, headed into the winter of 1940–41 with a government united by an uncomfortable, unwanted codependence.

By destroying Jewish businesses, along with seizing state-run monopolies for personal gain and murdering anyone who opposed them, the Iron Guard succeeded in throwing Romania's economy into complete disarray. Fear and civic chaos soon reigned throughout the land. Antonescu appealed to the Guard to change course for the good of the country, but he couldn't persuade them. The tension that had simmered between them was about to boil over. Antonescu knew he had to stop the Guard from driving Romania to total destruction, while the Legionnaires were so intoxicated with greed, so crazed for power, they were pumped for a confrontation.

On January 20, 1941, with Hitler's blessing, Antonescu made his move, dismissing the Legionnaires from the government. The

Iron Guard instantly revolted, and the insurrection swept through Romania like a tornado.

That same night, there was a knock on the door of Isadora's family's apartment. Adela opened it and found herself face-to-face with a teenage boy. His expression was strained, his eyes flashing with intensity, his panting breath turning to steam in the frigid air. It was Jonel, one of Isadora's friends, so Adela invited him in and offered to take his coat.

"No, thanks," he said. "I'm not staying long. I'm here to tell you that you have to hide. Do not leave the house tomorrow, and stay hidden until you know it's safe."

Isa, hearing the voice of her friend, came over to greet him. Sami and Dutsu, who had overheard what he said, gathered around to listen. Jonel was a Christian, and his father was an avowed anti-Semite and a high-ranking member of the Iron Guard. He had long discouraged Jonel from befriending Jews, but Jonel, remarkably, had proven immune to the disease of racial hatred. That evening, he had heard his father mirthfully going on about how the Jews were going to get what they deserved, and listened as his father told a friend that the Guard was about to turn Bucharest's Jewish neighborhoods—especially Dudesti—into graveyards.

"This is real," Jonel warned. "I don't care what you think you need to do tomorrow—do not go outside. Lock your doors and pretend you're not home. Better to maybe lose your jobs than your lives." With that, he left, saying he had a few more friends he had to warn. Adela had never liked the fact that Isadora spent time hanging around with the son of a known fascist; now, she was grateful.

Vili spread the word of the looming pogrom to their neighbors in the other units in their building. They all agreed to lock the outer gate of their shared courtyard once everyone was in for the night, and to lie low the next day, giving the impression that the building was vacant. Isa's family barred their door, moved blankets, pillows, water, and bread into a room without a window, and waited. They stayed there, leaving the room only to use the bathroom bucket, for the next three days.

Their precautions paid off—or perhaps they were just lucky that no one forced the gate to their home as the neighborhood was swept up in mayhem. They saw nothing, but heard the gunshots, the screams, the crashing glass. During those three days, 120 Jews would be murdered, and more than 1,100 beaten, raped, robbed, or otherwise molested—over 600 of whom lived in the Dudesti neighborhood. Houses were broken into and looted. Synagogues were burned. From the Great Pogrom, as it became known, came tales of gross humiliation: thirteen Jews were killed at a slaughter-house; some were disemboweled, hoisted up onto meat hooks, and labeled with signs that read KOSHER MEAT, as their intestines dangled onto the corpses on the floor below them. At a police station, a group of some 150 Jews were subjected to a mock trial, convicted of fantastic charges, flayed with a bullwhip, and then forced at gun-point to drink a concoction of magnesium salt, petroleum, gasoline, and vinegar. They were then locked in a tiny room and left to stew in their own shit and vomit until their tormentors became bored and released them.

By January 24, the army had shattered the Iron Guard. With no reliable party with whom to form a government, Antonescu installed a military dictatorship. "I am a dictator by fate," he said a few months later, "because I cannot return to the old constitution, the parlia-ment, nor to anything, and I can only solve [Romania's] problems with the State Council and some experts around me. . . ."

One of the problems he would energetically seek to solve was that of the so-called "Jewish question."

Despite the ousting of the Iron Guard, the Bucharest Pogrom seemed like only the beginning of worse to come. Isadora's family, and everyone else, knew Antonescu to be a confirmed anti-Semite, and his close relationship with Hitler dissuaded anyone from believing he'd ever be an ally to the Jews. The anti-Semitic laws passed a few months earlier had caused Anna to be fired from her teaching position, which only intensified her bouts of chronic depression. Then, a few weeks after the pogrom, Adela fell severely ill and died. It was the biggest blow of Isadora's young life, much more upsetting than even the loss of her father. Her grandmother had been more of a mother to her than Anna had been. She had made their tough life tolerable and was the solid foundation upon which the entire family was built. It was impossible for Isa to imagine a future without her; to this day, over sixty years later, when she speaks of her grandmother, she weeps.

Faced with the loss of their firm yet gentle matriarch, at a time when the fingers of terror were tightening around their people with no sign of loosening, Isadora's family felt like they were quickly running out of options. If they weren't murdered outright by fascists, they foresaw being pushed into utter destitution, even worse than the poverty in which they already lived. There was only one alternative: The family decided to move to the city of Balti (pronounced *Beltz*), in Bessarabia, where Isadora's aunt Mitzi lived. Since it was now in Soviet-controlled territory, out of the reach of Antonescu and the Romanian fascists, they were sure they'd be able to live in greater freedom and safety. It was the smartest thing they could have done under the circumstances. And it proved to be the worst of all possible decisions.

ELEVEN

In 1932, with the British restricting Jewish immigration to Palestine, Bela began leading illegal transports for eager Czech pioneers who didn't want to wait endlessly for permission. Since Jews were still allowed to visit the Holy Land, the immigrants traveled there in the guise of a tour group, with Bela as their guide. The British initially denied Bela's own request for a tourist visa after investigating his background, suspicious of his true motives, convinced he'd simply stay and settle. After much bureaucratic back-and-forth, they at last relented, on the condition that Bela leave his pregnant wife, his son, and a hefty cash bond at home, to ensure his return. They hadn't imagined that his real reason for going was to drop off a dozen people there—depositing them in the hands of ready Revisionist contacts who had arranged homes and jobs for them—before returning to Uzhgorod for more.

His first visit to the Land of Israel after over a decade of toiling for the Zionist cause left Bela with a deep sense of validation, mixed with some concern. He viewed the fruits of Jewish creativity with an almost religious awe and, though Palestine was still far from being able to function as an independent Jewish nation, Bela looked at the country in the same way a pragmatic dreamer looks at a run-down house, seeing the potential that could be achieved with the right kind of work. He was troubled, however, by the strong attachment to socialism held by many pioneers. Karl Marx and Josef Stalin, whose pictures were displayed throughout the land, seemed more admired than Herzl, and he saw as many flags featuring the hammer and sickle as the Star of David. He wasn't reflexively opposed to socialism, and had he believed it to be a sound ideology upon which to build the state, he would have supported it. But he was convinced that the practical drawbacks of building a new country on a socialist foundation outweighed its idealistic appeal.

Bela returned home more passionate than ever about training young people in the skills and values he thought would best serve the nascent Jewish homeland. He poured his energies into Uzhgorod's chapter of the Revisionists' Betar youth organization, which Joshua would soon be old enough to join. Bela took an ever-growing group of teenagers—both boys and girls—on camping trips in the Carpathian Mountains. They performed volunteer work in Uzhgorod, held monthly cultural events, and marched in parades. In preparation for self-defense in Palestine, boys were trained by Czech army soldiers to fire rifles and pistols. The teenagers were also indoctrinated with a code of honor, which promoted personal dignity, respect for others, service to the community and the Zionist cause, and a sense of the inherent value of being Jewish. They were like a Boy Scout unit with a political—and paramilitary—agenda.

A few months after Bela returned from his first trip to Palestine, Berta gave birth to their daughter, Aviva. It was almost exactly ten years since Joshua had been born, as Berta had accurately foretold. Joshua, whose excitement at the prospect of having a little brother or sister grew with Berta's belly through the pregnancy, was delighted with her arrival. His fondness for Aviva was instant and deep, and as she got older, he naturally adopted the role of protective big brother. As a young child, she was beautiful. Her cheeks were smooth and round, but not pudgy; her eyes were large, with irises nearly as dark as her pupils; her little lips were perfect, framed on either side by dimples, giving her an adorable smile. Her thick black hair was bobbed and parted from the left; as she got older, she grew it long and kept it in braids, of which she was understandably proud. Her ears may have been a little big for her head, and her teeth came in with some spaces between them, but these minor disproportions only gave her cuteness a touch of character. Bright, outgoing, and precocious, she was the kind of girl who easily won the affection of those who met her.

With an early attraction to acting, Aviva loved to perform for the other kids in their neighborhood. Joshua hammered together an improvised stage on the sidewalk for her, complete with a curtain. As a reward for good behavior, Berta took Aviva to see plays in Uzhgorod's theater, and, after each show she saw, Aviva begged to be taken to the stage door so she could see the actors in person. Once, the lead actor in a particular play, who came to recognize his little fan, approached Aviva, bowed, and kissed her hand. She was so giddy, she refused to wash it for a week.

Like any smart kid, Aviva used her talents to get what she wanted. Though Bela and Berta were immune to her manipulations, the other townspeople were not. She would sometimes return from school with candy or ice cream, which she had sweetly suckered some soft-hearted merchant into giving her. Later, when the war came and breadlines were common, Berta would send her out to bring back a loaf for the family; the last thing Aviva wanted to do with her day was waste it by standing in line, so she would stare with puppy-dog eyes at the others who were waiting, appearing to be on the verge of tears, and whimper to herself how she missed her mommy. Before long, the adults around her would melt and quickly usher her to the head of the line. Berta never understood how Aviva was able to bring back the bread so quickly, and Aviva never told, knowing her mother would disapprove of how she used her cleverness.

———◦◦◦———

Along with the weekly newspaper *Zsido Neplap*, Bela also published a literary journal every year just before Rosh Hashanah called, in English, *The Jewish Family Almanac*. The first few pages were devoted to a calendar, listing the days on which the holidays would fall, as well as the Torah portions for each week. The rest of the almanac, which some years ran over a hundred pages, was filled with essays, poems, songs, and even a few pages of Jewish jokes, such as this one:

> *On a train full of people, a group of anti-Semites were bad-mouthing the Jews. One of them was watching carefully to see how the Jews in the car would react. One Jew, maybe out of boredom or fatigue, started to yawn. The anti-Semite saw this, and said, "You'd love to swallow us all, wouldn't you?" The Jew protested, "God forbid—our Torah prohibits us from taking pleasure in pigs!"*

Bela himself wrote articles about his trips to Palestine, one-act plays, and paeans to Zionist heroes. In one issue, at the height of his war of words with Rabbi Shapira, Bela published a parable that was an obvious swipe at the ultra-Orthodox leader. In it Rabbi Levi Yitzhak of Berditchev—a great Hasidic master who had lived over a hundred years earlier, and about whom many legends were told—confronted Satan before the Heavenly Tribunal during Rosh Hashanah, as he did every year. Satan, as usual, presented a list of sins allegedly committed by the Jewish people and pressed the tribunal to condemn the Jews to oblivion. This particular year, the sins on the list were as numerous as grains of sand on a beach. Normally, Satan's accusations, despite being "painted with sulfur and tar," were easy to refute; but this time, when Rabbi Yitzhak and the other defenders of Israel protested against them, Satan replied: "I did not fabricate these charges, but your own pious rabbis did, and I introduce them as witnesses!"

As the others in the defense team stood speechless, Rabbi Yitzhak said, "We don't have to reflect on this that much; if God rips apart the devil who is the evil accuser, the accusations will disappear." The reply was "a blast of laughter bursting forth with sizzle and thunder from the mouth of the wicked Satan: 'Then you should rip apart your own rabbis,' he roared, while hot flames and vapors of tar escaped from his mouth. 'They are the ones who've made these charges against the good Children of Israel.' "

As the case for the Jews seemed dire, Rabbi Yitzhak saved the day by fervently praying the *Avinu Malkenu*, in which God is beseeched to silence the mouths of any false accusers. At the end of the tale, the great sage tells his disciples, "We have to avoid speaking evil about our brothers and sisters, and even more we have to avoid accusing them in front of our God. Satan is very good at creating false claims against the Children of Israel, and it's unnecessary for the Rabbis of Israel to help the Dark One in creating and listing all the claims and accusations against us, thereby becoming Satan's helping hands."

As the 1930s progressed and Bela's status as a Zionist leader rose, well-known authors from Czechoslovakia and abroad were drawn to contributing to the almanac, including Max Brod, the biographer and protégé of Franz Kafka. In 1935, Maxim Gorki, the Russian literary giant, contributed a piece scathing in its criticism of regimes that enflamed anti-Semitism to distract people from their daily misery, as well as the Gentiles who were successfully manipulated and the Jews whose solutions to their problems were ludicrously ineffective. Titled "Race Psychology," it reads:

Once upon a time, there were Jews living in a country—simple Jews who were needed for pogroms and accusations, which were required to maintain state security. When the population of that country began to complain about its situation, encouraging messages came from the lips of the officials charged with preserving order and peace: "People, have confidence in the authorities!"

The people assembled, and the distinguished gentlemen in power asked: "Why such worry?"

"Excellencies, gentlemen," the people responded, "we have no food to sink our teeth into!"

"And, do you still have some teeth?"

"We still have a few teeth . . ."

"Aha! So you have been concealing something from the authorities!"

And the authorities, judging that by smashing in the teeth of the people, they could snuff out their worries, resorted to this method without delay. When, however, they saw that this method was insufficient to ensure the necessary harmony to maintain their relationship with the citizens, they tried to resolve the matter through persuasion.

"So what is it you want?" they asked of the people.

"Land and bread!" most answered.

Others, however, who did not behave with any understanding of "state needs," had different ideas about what was needed to solve their problems: "It wouldn't do any harm to introduce an innovation . . . that a man could at least consider his teeth, cheeks, and innards as his own, and not be tortured without any reason whatever."

But the authorities interceded immediately and said to the people: "But brethren, what good are such dreams? Man does not live by bread alone, so say the Scriptures—and further: for each man beaten to death, we will spare two innocent ones."

"And those not in danger of being hurt agree to this?" the people asked dubiously.

"Of course! Therefore, put away your concerns. Instead, beat up on the Jews a little bit. What good are Jews for us anyway?"

The enlightened people began to think about it, and eventually realized that not being in a position to do anything smarter anyway than what the authorities had already decided, proclaimed, "Let's get to work, brethren, in the interest of the sacred goal!"

After they then burned down fifty Jewish homes and beat to death countless Jews, the people, tired from the work of maintaining state security, came to a different way of thinking. They gradually forgot what they had wanted, and the maintenance of order prevailed.

But the authorities discovered that beside the angered people and the beaten Jews, there still lived in the country some good-hearted souls, sixteen to be exact, who after every pogrom turned to the world's conscience with a written protest, stating that, "Although the Jews are also Russian citizens, we are nevertheless convinced that it is not correct to totally wipe them out, and therefore we condemn in the strongest terms the limitless murder of living people." Signed by sixteen friends of humanity, among them Grischa Budutschev, a seven-year-old child.

And so it came to be after each subsequent pogrom, with the only difference that Grischa continued to grow older.

While the Jews read these protesting writings, they sobbed even more bitterly, until one of them, who must have been a clever lad, made the following proposal: "Do you know what, my brothers? Before the next pogrom, we will hide all pens, paper, and ink, and then we'll see what these sixteen people do about it!"

And that is what they did, just like the lad said! The Jews bought up all the writing paper and pens, spilled all the ink into the sea, and then they waited for the next pogrom.

They didn't have to wait long: permission was requested, the pogrom was carried out and the hospitals filled up again with Jews with their heads beaten in and their bodies ravaged. . . . The friends of humanity ran all over Petersburg's every street, to look for pen, paper, and ink to write their protest, but all their efforts were in vain. They didn't find any anywhere, except perhaps in the offices of the authorities who, however, were not willing to give them any of it.

Grischa, who was forty-three years old by then, broke out in tears. "I want to protest!" But they found nothing on which to protest. Then one of them said, "Maybe on a plank or billboard?" And somewhere at the edge of town they found a ramshackle plank. But no sooner did one of them, using a piece of chalk, start to write a few words of protest on it, than a policeman came upon them and screamed at them. "What do you think you're doing? If schoolchildren do such a thing, they get spanked, but you are grown-ups. Aren't you ashamed?" The policeman had no idea what they were actually up to, but they, feeling ashamed, scattered and ran away.

That is how it came to happen that this time there was no protest against the pogrom, and the friends of humanity were left without satisfaction.

Those who understand the psychology of race are right: These Jews are clever people.

Fortunately for Joshua's family, the nightmares portrayed in the Gorki story bore no resemblance to their own situation. They continued to live openly and happily as Jews. "It was a good life then," my grandfather recalled. "We were free. As a family, we were close and content. We lived together in a kind of dream, the dream of Israel, and underneath everything coursed a sense of hope. As good as things were, there was the feeling that they were only going to get better." ☞

TWELVE

Everything changed in 1938.

The crack of thousands of boots slapping cobblestone in unison echoed down the streets of Uzhgorod. The angry clatter of tanks maneuvering into position shook the city like an earthquake. The Hungarians had come back.

With the signing of the Munich Pact on September 29, Hungary quickly sued to reclaim its former territories from Czechoslovakia. The two countries put the issue before Germany and Italy for binding arbitration, and on November 2, Hungary was awarded a long swath of land in southern Slovakia, plus a chunk of western Subcarpathia, including the cities of Uzhgorod and Mukacevo. Within a week, Hungarian troops had occupied the entire zone.

It was a couple of weeks before Joshua's sixteenth birthday when he watched the Hungarian army march into town. Curious throngs lined the streets to view the procession, greeting the soldiers neither as liberators nor as enemy oppressors. A few Hungarian nationals hung Hungarian flags in the windows of their homes and shops to welcome their countrymen, including a bookshop that had its windows broken by Czech patriots, but the scene was about as calm as it could have been.

Neither Joshua, nor his parents, nor anyone he can recall was too concerned about the occupation. Though many Jews were sad that Czechoslovakia, which had been so good to them, was disintegrating, anyone older than twenty remembered their lives under Hungarian rule as being quite tolerable. Many of them spoke Hungarian, had Hungarian friends and business associates, and had, like Bela, served in the Hungarian army. With the Germans encroaching on Czechoslovakia from the west, the realists knew it was far, far better to be in Hungarian hands than Hitler's.

But times had changed in Hungary. The country had been in dire economic straits for years, for which Jews provided a convenient scapegoat, even though the bulk of them were just as poor as their Christian neighbors. Jews were denounced in the press as unpatriotic parasites; ultra-right-wing groups—most notably the Arrow Cross, which received funding from Germany—whipped up riots against Jewish business owners, and influential church leaders preached aggressive solutions to the "Jewish question." By the late 1930s, finding an answer to this question became the country's overarching preoccupation.

The first in a series of anti-Semitic laws had been passed in May 1938. These new laws didn't apply to Jews who were decorated Hungarian war heroes, but Bela quickly learned that his medals wouldn't protect him. Within days of the occupation of Uzhgorod, soldiers arrived at his office with a sheaf of newspaper articles from 1930—some naming him as the leader of the movement that caused Hungarian to be replaced by Hebrew as one of the city's official languages, and others that Bela had written himself promoting the change. "You did this to us!" the Hungarians accurately asserted, and proceeded to exact their revenge.

Zsido Neplap was promptly shut down, never to produce another issue. Bela was roughed up, arrested, and jailed for a few days before being freed. It was only the beginning of a perpetual

campaign of harassment to which he was subjected over the following five-plus years, as he was repeatedly incarcerated and released.
Yet despite being a favorite target for the authorities, Bela pursued
his Zionist activities uninterrupted—minus the newspaper—continuing to vex the Hungarians.

Once, a few years after the occupation, Bela was taken to Budapest,
condemned to be held indefinitely at a prison for Jews, Communists,
and other untrustworthy elements. There was no trial, no charges
even brought against him, and no chance for him to exonerate himself.
Upon arriving in Budapest, as he was being led in handcuffs through the
train station, a well-dressed, dignified gentleman ran over, stopped the
guards, and asked what they thought they were doing. When the soldiers
explained that they were taking Bela to prison, the man who had intervened identified himself as the provincial governor of Subcarpathia. He
was an ethnic Ruthenian who knew Bela well, and who had little tol-
erance for Hungarian maltreatment of Jews in his jurisdiction. Within
an hour, he'd secured Bela's release, and soon the two traveled back
to Uzhgorod together. What seemed like good fortune, however, ultimately proved to be the opposite; when Hungarian Jews were eventually deported to concentration camps, by some quirk in the system the
inmates at the prison in which Bela was meant to be jailed were never
sent to Auschwitz, and hence survived the war.

For about six months after the Hungarians occupied Uzhgorod,
Bela was permitted to continue running his commercial printing
business. Then, on May 4, 1939, Hungary passed the Second Anti-
Jewish Law. The business licenses of Jews were revoked, they were
forbidden from teaching in or attending public schools, and banned
from voting or holding public office, producing plays and films, and
buying and selling land.

Like just about every other Jewish merchant in Subcarpathia,
Bela handed his business over to a "straw man," a Gentile who acted

as a front for Jewish shop owners. Fortunately he had trustworthy friends in the Christian community, so he had no trouble finding a buyer who'd hire him as an employee and share the print shop's profits with him. Many Jews throughout the region, however, signed their livelihoods over to straw men only to find themselves robbed of all the profits and either paid a pittance for their labor or fired outright, casting many middle-class Jews into destitution.

Uzhgorod's impressive Hebrew high school, which Joshua attended and Bela had crisscrossed the continent collecting donations to build, was seized by the Hungarian army to house its administrative offices. Yet the school, as an entity, wasn't outlawed, and as Jewish students were thrown out of state schools, the numbers who enrolled at the Hebrew high school more than doubled. Since Jewish professors had lost their university posts, they flocked to jobs at the Hebrew school, raising the caliber of education higher than it had ever been before. The school was set to flourish, if only a building could be found by autumn to accommodate the students. The religious Jewish community refused to help the Zionists in any way, and all city-owned buildings were off-limits. Bela worked his many connections and tried calling in favors from Gentile politicians whom he'd helped in the past, but it seemed no one was in a position to do anything. As summer wore on, the situation appeared bleak. At last, the bishop of the Greek Catholic Church, Alexander Stojka, came to the rescue, offering the Zionists use of the church's seminary as a schoolhouse.

When lessons began in the fall, an aura of excitement filled the classrooms. So much was new—the setting, many of the students and teachers, and the world that was changing around them. The anti-Jewish measures aroused their sense of cultural pride and imbued the Zionist program with pressing relevance. Scorned by the Hungarians, rejected by their Orthodox brethren, the students were filled with a sense of unity, bonded by the glue of adversity and injustice. They were all young enough to have been born Czech citizens, and they yearned as much for their former country and its freedoms as they did for a Jewish homeland in Palestine. But neither they, nor anyone else, imagined the situation would get any worse, and they made the best of it. For Joshua, and many of his teenage peers, the most exciting thing about the new school was that there were more girls to look at.

With the outbreak of World War II, Hungary, like Romania and other smaller powers, feared being crushed between Hitler and Stalin if it remained unallied. Regent Miklos Horthy, figuring that his country had a better chance of retaining its sovereignty if it sided with the Germans, officially joined the Axis in November 1940. Meanwhile, the rights of Hungarian Jews continued to erode. Under the rationale that they were "alien elements," every Jew was required to prove that their family had lived on Hungarian soil prior to 1868—the year that all minorities had been granted equal status under Hungarian law. Those that couldn't were stripped of their citizenship and could be expelled from the country at any time, for any reason.

Bela sent his son on a mission to dig up some evidence that would prove their generational ties to Hungary. By this time, Joshua had become a lean young man, with taut, olive-skinned cheeks, full lips, and penetrating eyes peering from behind round, tortoiseshell glasses. On a sunny morning in early June, he hitchhiked to the town of Hunkovce, about ten miles west of Uzhgorod, where his grandfather Jozsef was born. Though his task was a serious one, he figured he might as well enjoy himself, so he let the few cars on the road pass him by, preferring instead to ride in horse-drawn wooden carts driven by peasants, who he thanked with cigarettes that he'd bought for this purpose. In a few hours, after switching carts a few times, he arrived at his grandfather's village, and got out in front of the house where Bela's half-sister Malvin and her children Blanca, Bill, and Ilona lived.

Malvin promptly sat him down at the kitchen table and stuffed him with carrot salad, borscht, and fried potatoes, until he could no longer obey her commands to eat, eat. When Joshua was finally allowed to excuse himself, Bill, who was about Joshua's age, but a little shorter, stockier, and with that healthy glow that rural life often bestows on young men, took Joshua to find the oldest people in town—two brothers, both in their nineties, who lived next door to each other.

As they approached the houses, they saw one of the brothers sitting in a chair under a shady bower in his courtyard. They knocked on the gate and were invited to enter, and Bill, who was acquainted with the old man, introduced Joshua. The man welcomed him with a toothless grin spread across a face as creased and hard as a walnut. Explaining why he had come, Joshua said he was the grandson of Jozsef Szrulovits, and asked if by chance the old man might remember Jozsef's father.

"Remember him?" countered the old man, whose wits were still perfectly sharp. "I couldn't forget him if I wanted to. And my brother will surely remember him, too." He agreed to get his brother and walk over to the notary's office to give a sworn statement saying that Joshua's family had lived there prior to 1868.

A simple statement wasn't enough. The notary had apparently been advised to treat Jews attempting to prove their heritage with suspicion, in case they simply bribed someone to testify on their behalf. So he asked the old men to describe Joshua's great-grandfather. He was a farmer, they said, who also rented a small mill where villagers brought corn and wheat to be ground. He was huge and powerfully built, able to carry two bags of flour—one over each shoulder—at the same time. And they were intimately familiar with his strength. Once, when they were young, they stole some corn from Joshua's great-grandfather's field. He had caught them in the act and came after them, they said, and they trembled as they recounted running away in terror through the cornstalks, the long green leaves slapping their faces. "It was like being chased by a monster," the older brother said.

"I fell," said the younger brother, "and my brother stopped to pick me up. That's when he caught us. . . ." The brothers, some eighty years after it took place, looked at each other in front of Joshua, Bill, and the notary, and burst into tears as they described the beating they'd received from Joshua's great-grandfather. Joshua, startled by their emotional recollection, hesitatingly apologized for the actions of an ancestor he never knew. "No, no, we did deserve it," the elder brother said, as he collected himself, "and I tell you, we never stole again." The notary couldn't help but be convinced of the old men's candor, and Joshua went back to Uzhgorod with the paper that would spare his family from the threat of deportation.

Jews who couldn't find nanogenarian witnesses had to produce tax records or other official documentation showing their families' presence on Hungarian soil over seventy years earlier. This involved bureaucratic sleuthing that many Jews couldn't afford. Most simply ignored the rule out of a sense of complacency. The threat of deportation struck them as absurd: In the first place, everyone in each community knew where everyone else was from, and besides— who was really going to deport them, and to where?

On June 22, 1941, Germany launched Operation Barbarossa, simultaneously invading the Soviet Union at multiple points along its frontier. Five days later, Hungary declared war on Russia and committed troops to the Axis offensive. By early July, German and Hungarian troops had advanced deep into Ukraine. Soon after, the deportations from Subcarpathia began.

Around 20,000 Jews who couldn't prove their generational ties to Hungary were rounded up and sent over the Ukrainian border to Kamenetz-Podolsk, where they were handed over to a Nazi SS division. At the end of August, the unlucky Subcarpathians, along with thousands of local Ukrainian Jews, were ordered into a massive pit. The SS, standing on the rim, unleashed a thunderstorm of machine-gun fire. The pit was so full of people that some weren't even hit by bullets, but smothered to death beneath the bodies of others. Over a period of two days, more than 23,000 Jews were slaughtered.

A fortunate few, whom the bullets had missed and who had been able to breathe beneath the sea of corpses, escaped once it was safe to slip from the cover of the carnage. Naturally, they told their story to anyone who would listen. By the end of September, word of the massacre had reached Uzhgorod. No one believed it. It was written off as a wild rumor spread by agitators, since it was obviously too impossible to be true. Soon after, a couple of Polish Jews who had escaped from the clutches of the Nazis made their way to Uzhgorod. They sought out the leaders of Uzhgorod's religious Jewish community, to tell them about the hundreds of thousands of displaced Jews in Poland who were starving in sealed ghettos, in cities like Warsaw and Lodz. Their report wasn't believed either, their warnings were dismissed, and they were urged to keep their ridiculous story to themselves, so as not to cause a panic. Rejected by the rabbis, the Poles were advised to talk to Bela. On their way to his print shop, they were astonished, and enraged, at the sight of Jews simply going about their business as usual. By the time they reached the print shop, the Poles could hardly contain themselves.

"What is going on in this town?" one of the men exclaimed. "Are you people all crazy? The world is burning and you live here like nothing's happening!"

THIRTEEN

I took the train south from Uzhgorod into Hungary, then transferred to an east-bound line that crossed the border into Romania. Summer abruptly turned to autumn, bringing with it cold rain and soupy fog. The next few days were spent in transit, alternating between lumbering public buses and minivans bulging with passengers who insisted on keeping every window sealed tight—as though they had a phobia of fresh air, a total disregard for germ theory, or a love of the steamy aromas of others. Hitchhiking, a common practice in Romania, quickly became my preferred mode of getting around as I cut across the northern part of the country. Heavy clouds blanketed the mountains and filled the valleys; rain splattered on car windows and trickled across them in erratic trails. I was in a gray traveler's purgatory, moving, but with little visual evidence of actually getting anywhere.

Entering the province of Maramures, the sun punched through the mist, illuminating rolling hills that were carved into fields, pastures, and orchards, looking like a giant rumpled quilt stitched from patches every shade of green. The region has a reputation as a kind of "Land that Time Forgot," where people live much the way they did hundreds of years ago. And it's partly true. Peasant women in babushkas and rubber boots scrape the earth with hoes, turning up potatoes. With their black pleated skirts, black blouses, and shrunken-apple faces, they evoke the Baba Yaga or any other witch from the old stories. Men with long gleaming scythes clear acres of waist-high grasses, which are piled into haystacks so big—with round sides and pointed peaks—they look like primitive dwellings dotting the landscape like a thatch city. Other men chop firewood in pairs, one steadying a maul atop a round of wood while his partner swings down upon it a boulder lashed to the end of a stick. Everyone's hands are rough and indelibly dirty. Teeth are stained or missing.

Plenty of folks still live in their ancestral wooden houses, which are like log cabins built on stone foundations, with peaked tin roofs and porches strung with *ristras* of onions and garlic and bean pods. Cows, pigs, and chickens fill muddy courtyards and wander freely down the streets. Horses pulling wagons clop by in cleated shoes that probably provide great traction in the fields but look danger-ously unsure as they scrape the pavement. Centuries-old wooden churches, with towering pointed steeples covered with shingles that look like fish scales, rise beside cemeteries with eroded headstones.

But time is remembering this place pretty quickly. Cars dart around horses on the road. Right next to the quaint wooden cot-tages sit garish cinder-block boxes. Every house has electricity; many have phones, and some have satellite dishes. Still, it seemed like it might be the best place in the country to get a living sense of traditional Romanian life, and worth a stop on the way to the town further east where my grandmother had been born.

I found a village in which the old ways were still stronger than the new, evidenced by the fact that there were about twenty horses on the main street for every car. Small signs hung on a number of houses, advertising rooms for rent to tourists, so I chose one more or less at random—fifteen dollars a night for a bed and two huge meals a day. The walls of the modern two-story home were covered with kitschy Christian iconography; above my bed hung a painting of Baby Jesus on Mary's lap in heaven, gazing down upon sinners pleading for mercy while reaching desperately up from a fiery inferno. Behind the house was a small wooden barn, a garden with a few rows each of corn, squash, potatoes, and cabbage, a pen that held three white ducks, and a plum orchard that spread up a steep hillside. Grapevines climbed lattice arbors near a picnic table.

The owner of the house was fat man with a bald pate, thin mats of gray hair sprouting on the sides of his head, and a couple days' growth of stubble covering his jowls. He wore a blue polyester tracksuit jacket over a yellow polo shirt. His name was Gheorgie, and his manner was jocular and fraternal. He spoke French, which proved to be a mixed blessing: While it made communication simple, I soon discovered that I'd surely settled into the home of the most talkative man in Romania, and I couldn't feign ignorance when I wearied of his chatter. His meek, white-haired wife seemed to live in the kitchen, and his daughter, home from university on break to help with the harvest, was usually out in the fields somewhere.

After showing me the house, Gheorgie and I stood by the picnic table in the yard. He boasted proudly of his satellite dish. His favorite show, he said, was *Dallas*, and he launched into a mirthful explanation of the rivalry between J.R. and Bobby. I couldn't help thinking that perhaps this *was* the Land that Time Forgot.

"Come," he said, "let me introduce you to my best friend," and began walking to the barn. He swung open the chicken-wire gate to the sloppy barnyard, and I followed him inside. Then he opened the barn's wooden door and, grinning, said, "There he is!" I found myself face-to-face with an enormous, snorting, shit-stained pig. "He's like my twin," said Gheorgie, laughing, as he patted his own huge belly. "He's only got a few more months to go; then we'll eat him for Christmas and I'll have to find another friend." His affection for the beast was genuine, but something told me that not even a miraculous weaving spider was going to keep this pig off the table.

Next to the barn were a few wooden vats so large, a man—even Gheorgie—could drown in them. Each was covered with plastic sheeting, which was weighted down by a couple of boards. He used them for making plum brandy, of which he said he produced over 1,000 liters a year, and claimed to drink every drop. "I'll bring some now," he said. "Sit at the table and I'll be right back." It was mid-afternoon, but anytime was the right time to drink in this household. He brought a glass decanter filled with clear liquid to the picnic table. "Romanian whiskey! Good for your health!" he pronounced, and poured us each a shot. Not usually a big drinker, I slugged back the *slivovitz* out of politeness. It was firewater, scalding the throat on the way down. The moment I put the glass on the table it was refilled, so I gulped it down, then kept hold of the glass until the cork was back on the bottle.

In the meantime, Gheorgie asked me where in America I lived and about my family. I told him about my home, and showed him pictures of my family. He looked them over one by one, and asked if my parents also lived in New Mexico. "No," I said, "they live in New York."

A pensive look crossed Gheorgie's face. "New York, New York," he muttered. "The mayor there is Bloomberg, yes? Bloomberg. That sounds like the name of a Jew. Is Bloomberg a Jew?" he asked. "Like Henry Kissinger? Like Senator Lieberman? Like Madeleine Albright?"

At the first mention of the word *Jew*, a yellow flag went up in my mind. By the time he reached Madeleine Albright, of all people, internal alarm bells were ringing. *You have got to be keeping a list to remember that she is Jewish*, I thought.

"I—I'm not really sure if Bloomberg is Jewish," I answered. "I think he is."

"I've heard," he went on, "that the Jews—you know, those people with the long beards and the black hats—had ten tons of gold stashed beneath the World Trade Center when it collapsed. . . ." He didn't bother to spell out what that meant to him, but it plainly wasn't good. I was suddenly very glad that I'd thought to crop the menorah out of the photo I'd brought of my sister and her son.

Though it was slightly unsettling to realize I'd just taken a room in the home of a probable anti-Semite, I'd traveled extensively in Arab countries, so was familiar with hiding my identity as a Jew, even among people I interacted with daily for months on end. Having never blown my cover before, I knew I could keep it here. Besides, the door to my bedroom could be bolted from the inside.

I told Gheorgie I was going to walk around for a while, and he asked if seven o'clock would be a good time for dinner. I said sure, then climbed the high hill behind the house to get a feel for my surroundings. With views of distant villages scattered among fields and foothills, clustered around white churches with prominent steeples, the landscape was reminiscent of New England, but with a bigger sky and less cluttered with trees. Imagining what Gheorgie would've been like if he'd lived sixty-five years earlier, I doubted it would have taken much to turn him into a Legionnaire.

By the time I got back to the house, darkness was falling. My host was delighted to see me, since dinner was ready: a feast of chicken soup, cabbage salad, potatoes, beans, and pork, along with a shot of plum brandy. While talking as CNN reports about Hurricane Rita flashed across the television, I learned that Gheorgie was a middle school math teacher. He spoke with rough affection for his students, like you might expect from a football coach, and said he pressed them hard, for their own good.

"I hung a sign in the classroom, which is like my motto," he said. "It reads *Work Makes You Free*."

I pondered that for a moment before he continued.

"It's the same as on the sign that Hitler hung over the entrance to Auschwitz. You know—Hitler, Hitler? Auschwitz?"

"Yes," I assured him. I knew them both.

FOURTEEN

Balti was a modest Bessarabian city situated in a broad grassy basin, a small urban island rising amid a sea of farmland. Seeking shelter from the storm of anti-Semitism raging in Romania, Isadora and her family moved there, descending upon her aunt Mitzi. They tried to piece together a new life with as much optimism as can be mustered by those who have struggled not to achieve their dreams, but only to keep them from slipping forever below the distant horizon.

Isadora and Yisrael enrolled in school and made friends, adapting easily to their new home. Mitzi, who was a highly respected French teacher, used her influence to secure a good teaching job for Anna. Renee was hired as a jeweler's assistant. Sami and Vili found work in a bakery, Dutsu in a hardware store; nothing to brag about, but earning better salaries than they had in Bucharest. Though the two-room house they shared was cramped, everyone except Mitzi was already accustomed to living atop one another, and any inconveniences she suffered were offset by her relief at knowing her family was safe. Balti was free from terror and violence and felt ripe with possibilities. They began to believe that they'd left their troubles behind in Bucharest.

Life seemed perfectly normal to Isadora, in the best of ways—her days were filled with studying, helping around the house, and going to the movies whenever she got the chance and had the money. The Jews and Gentiles of Balti mingled freely with one another, and Isa had more friends who weren't Jewish than who were. Though there were many more horses and carts than motorcars on the streets, the sidewalks were lined with shops, banks, and restaurants; Isadora, now sixteen years old, began to thrive in a city just vibrant and sophisticated enough to be exciting, yet small and simple enough to feel homey. She'd become a beautiful young woman, with soft ivory cheeks, a perfect nose, and large, sparklingly expressive eyes that naturally conveyed her inner goodness. By this time, she could switch between Romanian and French as nimbly as a goat can pivot on a cliff, and she'd begun to learn some Russian, though in that language, she was about as agile as a barge. She'd decided to become a teacher when she got older, like her mother and her aunt.

Within months, however, Operation Barbarossa engulfed Bessarabia. Romania had joined forces with Germany, offering its territory as a staging ground for the invasion of Ukraine and sending troops into battle alongside German armies. As thanks, Hitler pledged to return to Romania the provinces of Bessarabia and Bukovina, which had to be retaken from the Soviets before the Axis armies could penetrate the southern Ukrainian frontier.

By early July 1941, Balti was rocked by aerial assaults. Firebombs rained from above each afternoon for days on end, smashing homes into flaming heaps of rubble, leveling most of the city's buildings. Unextinguished pyres lapped at the sky, illuminating the night with an infernal light, filling the streets with an acrid haze. The blasts of heavy guns grew louder in the west, approaching like slow-moving thunder. The most nervous residents hastily packed a few bags and fled deeper into Soviet territory as the Red Army retreated. Others abandoned the city for nearby rural villages. But many stayed, hoping their fortunes would ride the crest of the wave of war that swept toward them. When the air-raid sirens wailed, Isadora and her family huddled together in their basement, feeling the shudder of each explosive tremor, praying they wouldn't be obliterated from above. It was like living through the Bucharest pogrom all over again, but worse. By July 10, Balti was in German hands. Isadora's family knew it would be bad for the Jews, but they couldn't imagine just how bad.

They'd heard rumors of a recent pogrom perpetrated by soldiers and ordinary citizens in the Romanian city of Iasi fifty miles to the south, just west of the Bessarabian border. But the stories that had seeped out of that cultured metropolis of universities, parks, theaters, and businesses were of such inconceivable proportions that the Jews of Balti were sure they'd been grossly exaggerated. They hadn't been; between June 27 and June 30, some 13,000 Jews had been slaughtered there. Among them were 4,500 souls packed into boxcars on "death trains" that trundled aimlessly on the tracks for a week with no food, no water, no ventilation, and no destination, under a searing summer sun. Even when the trains occasionally stopped, guards refused to open the doors to give the prisoners air. People were crammed inside too tightly to move, in brain-baking, suffocating heat, nauseated by the fetor of shit, piss, and death. Most of the prisoners died or went insane.

In subsequent days, as the Axis armies advanced on Balti, they blazed a trail marked with Jewish bodies: 800 massacred in Noua Sulita, 500 in Edineti, over 1,000 in Marculesti, and many more throughout the countryside. Groups of Jews fleeing one village for another, caught on the road by Romanian soldiers, were marched into swamps or to the lips of antitank ditches and gunned down. Some had to watch as their children's faces were smashed to pulp by rifle butts. Some women were spared, if you can call it that, and enslaved in brothels that served the German troops.

After the occupation of Balti, Jews in the city were shot at random, ten here, fifty there. But it was safer than in the countryside, so Jews flocked to the city from all directions. They were quartered in a makeshift ghetto in a public square outside the Bank of Moldova, along with the Jewish residents of Balti whose homes were destroyed in the air raids. A council of Jewish leaders was formed to help tend to the needs of those in the ghetto, and to this committee the Germans submitted a demand that twenty alleged Jewish Communists be turned over for execution. If the accused were not delivered, many more Jews, starting with the committee members themselves, would be killed. The committee unanimously refused to capitulate.

Its members were tortured and humiliated by German soldiers, then taken, along with forty-six others, to a quarry outside of Balti. After being forced at gunpoint to dig their own graves, each was shot in the neck. Only one was spared—a man by the name of Bernard Walter, who had once been Balti's assistant mayor—thanks to the appeals of his good friend, the city's Romanian police chief.

Isadora's family was among those who weren't ghettoized since their house had survived the invasion, and keeping their home was their one consolation as the world quickly crumbled around them. Isa's uncles rarely went out for fear of being shot; Anna and Mitzi were forced from their teaching positions and pressed into menial service in one of the German army kitchens; Renee was taken on as a maid in German headquarters. Throughout the city, there was a sense of anticipation. Everything was in flux. Maybe the Germans would move on, Isadora reasoned, deeper into Russia, leaving Balti in the dust of their tank treads and forgetting about it. If so, might life return to normal? The news from Bucharest was that things had calmed down there; perhaps the same could occur in Balti. She hoped to be able to start school again in the fall.

But the conversations among the grown-ups in her family made such a sunny outcome seem unlikely. One of the German officers for whom Renee worked had told her, in the vaguest of terms, that life for the Jews was only going to get worse. He himself wasn't anti-Semitic, at least by Nazi standards, and he sympathized with Renee's plight. Unable to protect her entire family, he offered to shelter Isadora. She was blonde, after all, and could easily masquerade as a Gentile. "I could walk her in front of Hitler and he'd never guess she was Jewish," the officer proclaimed.

Renee discussed the idea with Anna and Mitzi. As logically as they could in a time devoid of reason, they weighed the risks of various scenarios. Though she felt it would tear her in two to part with her daughter, Anna concluded that, in the end, Isadora would probably be safest under the care of the German. But when the choice was presented to her, Isadora rejected it. Whatever was to befall them, she preferred to stick with her family than to be handed over to a strange man, however well-intentioned he might be.

About six weeks after the Germans arrived, in the last days of August, there was a knock on the door. Two men, Jews from Balti who were among those chosen for the new leadership committee, stood on the threshold. Orders had been given, they said, and all Jews were being moved from the town to work for the Germans somewhere else. They didn't know where, or what kind of work they'd be asked to perform. Everyone was instructed to pack only what they could carry with them and gather by the ghetto in front of the bank. No, they had no more information, they said when Dutsu began to question them, and they had to be getting on to deliver the news to others.

Isadora's family anxiously packed a few small bags, one of which was filled with a large down comforter that compressed easily. After a debate over what to do with the family's jewelry, Sami and Dutsu dug a hole in the yard and buried the few pieces that had the most sentimental value. The rest they decided to take with them. It wasn't much to carry, anyway. Meanwhile, Anna sat Isadora down on a stool, pulled out a pair of scissors, and told Yisrael to bring his sister one of his shirts and a pair of his pants.

"Mom, what are you doing?" Isadora asked.

"I'm turning you into a boy," Anna replied.

"But—"

"No 'buts,' " Anna said. "This is for your own good—at least until we know it's safe."

Isadora sat still and silent as her mother chopped her tresses into a crew cut. Then she tried on her brother's clothes and scrutinized herself in the mirror. The clothes were a little baggy, but fit well enough. With her shorn hair and skinny, curveless body, she was convincing. She stood there for a moment, eyes glued to her reflection. Who was this person staring back at her, and what was going to happen to him? She felt empty, shaken out of herself by the impact of the unknown.

The town square was bustling with thousands of Jews, from the newborn to the elderly, with bags and bundles tightly held. The perimeter was ringed by Romanian soldiers and Germans in the unmistakable uniforms of the SS, who kept a dispassionate eye on the crowd. Isadora and her family waited among them for hours, as anxiety paled to boredom. At last, a voice was broadcast over a loudspeaker, telling the Jews they were being relocated for their own safety. They were going to walk to their destination— which remained unnamed—and no one would be permitted to lag behind. The Jews were split into groups a few thousand strong, and orders were given to move out.

FIFTEEN

With Bessarabia and Bukovina back in Romanian hands, Antonescu rapidly implemented plans to "cleanse the earth" in the provinces, by killing or deporting every Jew who lived there. Those who weren't murdered on the spot were to be marched in convoys into Transnistria, a swath of Ukraine bordering Bessarabia to the east, just over the Dniester River. Gifted to Romania by Germany after the Axis forces swept into the Soviet Union, Transnistria was initially meant to be a temporary holding ground for the deported Jews. Later, according to the plans, they would be transferred even further east, over the River Bug, out of Transnistria and into German hands. There, they would be used for slave labor or target practice, or whatever else the Germans fancied; Antonescu didn't care, as long as they were out of his domain. "If circumstances permit, they will be driven beyond the Urals," Antonescu told his cabinet members in the fall of 1941. "Pack them into the catacombs, throw them into the Black Sea," he wrote a few weeks later to his appointed governor in Transnistria. "[As far as I'm concerned,] 100 can die, 1,000 can die, all of them can die."

First, however, Transnistria had to be groomed to accept the more than 100,000 Jews soon to enter it. This required ghettoizing or exterminating the existing Jewish population of the region, which numbered some 300,000 before the war, about half of whom withdrew deeper into Ukraine along with the Soviet army. Of the 150,000 remaining in Transnistria in August 1941, perhaps 800 were still alive by 1943. In Odessa, tens of thousands were slain over the course of a week: 5,000 were hung in the city's main square; many more than that were herded into the countryside and locked inside wooden barns, which were machine-gunned from the outside, then incinerated with kerosene and grenades. Those who weren't murdered outright died slow and miserable deaths in ghetto camps along the River Bug, where, according to one Romanian officer, a dog's life was worth more than a Jew's.

Eager to commence with the purification of Bessarabia, Antonescu ordered the first convoys of Jews to cross the Dniester at the end of July 1941, before the Germans officially relinquished Transnistria to Romanian authority. The Germans, totally unprepared to deal with 25,000 bedraggled deportees in newly occupied terrain, refused to keep them. A standoff ensued between German and Romanian commanders, each trying to offload the Jews on the other. The people in the convoys, given neither food nor shelter, were detained on the riverbanks, marched back and forth along the roads, and prodded over the Dniester numerous times. Thousands were shot or died from exhaustion, sickness, and starvation. The deportation plans, which had been laid out systematically on paper, were in tatters from day one. ⊂═══⊸

SIXTEEN

The throng of thousands was herded from the center of Balti to the city limits and beyond. Some carried suitcases, others hefted bundles tied with string on their backs. Head-scarved women cradled infants or held the hands of their children. The long beards of men were tossed over their shoulders by the wind. A warm drizzle fell from an ominous sky, causing eyes to squint against the splatter and clothing to darken, drop by drop. Snaking in long lines along the country roads, between vast fields of sunflowers and corn, past empty plots of tilled earth the color of coffee, the sad parade was struck dumb, gagged by the heavy hand of the unknown. The only sounds were those of fabric rustling against fabric, footsteps slapping puddles, and caustic commands from the soldiers ordering their human herd to keep moving or be shot. Even the babies knew to be silent.

Isadora, trying to act like the boy she appeared to be, trudged beside her brother, surrounded by her family. Despite the precautionary change of identity, her mother had assured her that everything would be all right, that where they were going would be safer for them than Balti had been. Isadora clung to those words, wanting to believe them, but she had never been particularly brave and felt hardly older than a child. Her strongest solace came from the faces of her uncles, and her aunt Mitzi, who remained calm yet alert.

They marched without stopping, expected to maintain a soldier's well-trained pace. As the afternoon wore on, becoming a light-headed dream, the first pangs of hunger struck. Dutsu tore pieces from a loaf of bread he'd carried under his shirt, to keep it from getting soggy, and passed them around. Long accustomed to having little to eat, Isadora was satisfied for a while. Maybe they didn't have too far to go, she reasoned; she had no idea, so why imagine the worst? Maybe everything *would* be fine. It had always worked out that way for Shirley Temple. A ray of optimism shone within her, lightening her steps, even as her shoes grew heavier with mud. She realized that if everyone outside the family was to believe she was a boy, she'd need a boy's name. She broke the silence.

"Call me Mihai," she said.

Her family turned to look at her, and Mitzi, understanding instantly, started to laugh. "Okay, *boychik*," she said. "Mihai it is."

With the shroud of gloom temporarily lifted, the family bantered among themselves. They'd had plenty of practice making the best of tough times together. Yisrael even dared to speak half-jokingly of the future, suggesting as he often had before that maybe, when they got where they were going, they could finally get a dog.

As evening approached, the clouds began to part. Pools of purple and rose swirled overhead, and a weak golden light seeped across the western sky. The convoy came to a halt near the edge of a small village. Peering ahead to see what was going on, Isadora noticed a few of the soldiers talking to a couple of peasants, motioning toward their partially harvested cornfield. One peasant assessed the line of rain-drenched refugees, turned to look at his field himself, then continued his conversation with the soldiers. From their body language, Isadora was sure they were haggling over something, like they were in a market. A few moments later, with an apparent agreement struck, the soldiers motioned to three of the Jews nearest them to step forward. Two men and a woman. One of the soldiers pulled his pistol from his holster and shot them each once in the head. The bodies collapsed, spraying mud and water where they fell. A collective gasp like a quick loud breath taken before diving underwater rose from those who were close enough to see. Isadora, terrified, looked up at her uncle Dutsu, who hugged her tightly to him.

The soldiers, using their rifles like shepherd's staffs, ordered the Jews into the field. This was where they were going to spend the night. The column filed off the road and down into the dirt, as the peasants stripped the murdered Jews of their clothing, their shoes, and their bags. The rent had thus been paid. None of the Jews dared approach the corpses to bury them. The soldiers and the peasants couldn't be bothered. The bodies remained on the side of the road, naked carrion.

Standing in the soggy field, with the fading light creating the illusion that Isadora was looking at the world through a hazy window, reality hit hard. The mud would be their bed, as though they were a bunch of pigs. No one was going to feed them or even give them water. And death could come, for her or anyone in her family, at any moment, capricious and swift. Dutsu, Vili, and Sami collected as many dead cornstalks as they could and spread them over the ground, upon which the weary family laid down. Isadora nestled against her mother, sobbing herself quietly into a damp and fitful sleep. ⊙——‹›-

SEVENTEEN

The days pass and turn to weeks. Every morning, marching. Every evening, sleeping under open skies or, if lucky, in a barn. Clothing frays and tears, grows baggy on bodies shrinking from starvation. Shoes disintegrate. Feet swell and blister and bleed. Skin darkens with dirt. Eyes dim into blank vacancy, as though the souls to which they are the windows have gone into hibernation.

The roads are so saturated that with each step, Isadora sinks to her knees in mud, which sucks at her legs like it's trying to swallow her. Her weakened muscles resist with a will of their own, somehow managing to extract her feet from the mire, over and over and over again. She's seen what happens to those who no longer have the strength to fight it: the children who fall, whose parents don't have the strength to lift them; the elderly, the exhausted, the sick, who collapse and cease to struggle. Some are shot, like horses, yet with less dignity. Others are simply left to die. Each day, bodies are abandoned along the road in ever greater numbers, where they are picked clean of their belongings by local people, some of whom stand patiently along the roadside, watching without expression, smoking cigarettes, waiting to swoop in like human vultures on the freshly dead.

When she's thirsty, Isadora pauses for a moment to drink from a murky puddle. She's always hungry, yet trains herself to eat slowly, one bite at a time, from a raw onion, a still-dirty potato, a piece of bread, each morsel purchased by an uncle from peasants who bring baskets to the roadside. She sees her mother's necklace traded for four loaves of bread; a silver ring that her grandmother had worn is now worth a cabbage and a few potatoes; her long-dead father's old pocket watch, which was his father's before him and should have one day gone to Yisrael, is passed on to a stranger, converted into onions and turnips. After the first couple of transactions, any pangs of nostalgia or remorse are erased by an all-consuming desperation for food; the only regret is having buried some of the jewelry in the yard and not having it on hand to trade. The family tries to budget their valuables, a virtual impossibility, since they don't know how long they'll be on the move; the best they can do is spend them as sparingly as possible, supplementing what they buy with what they surreptitiously gather from the fields in which they sleep.

After a couple of weeks, typhus and dysentery rage through the convoy. Skeletal apparitions dressed in rags, delirious with fever, soiled with their own feces, slip and stumble forward, driven on only by the most animal of instincts. Some, no longer able to walk, bribe the soldiers to let them ride in one of the four horse-drawn supply carts; the soldiers take the gold or the jewels and hoist the infirm into the wagons, where they remain for a few days, heaped among other cadaverous figures. They inevitably die and are pitched unceremoniously to the ground.

Each day melds into the next, a monotonous nightmare punctuated with moments of violence and terror. Isadora loses track of time and place as the convoy marches circuitously, toward no discernible goal. The countryside itself offers few clues as to where they are. A gently rolling landscape that is rarely flat, the road traverses long, gradual inclines that merge into long, gradual descents. The views are vast, the sky huge, yet all there is to see is one massive, grassy swale of earth succeeding the next, converging in creases cut by intermittent creeks. The hillsides are faintly scarred by sheep trails, and sometimes shepherds appear, tall wooden staffs in hand, leading their flocks. "I would rather be a sheep in that herd," thinks Isadora when she sees one, "than a person in this one. At least they have plenty to eat."

Farmers are in the fields, turning up potatoes and turnips with hoes, picking corn, hanging tobacco to dry on wooden scaffolds. Horses stand idly, flicking their tails, hitched to carts being loaded with the harvest. Outside houses in the villages they pass, wood is being chopped and stacked, readied for winter. Even Isadora, whose mind has by now mastered the art of disassociation, is flabbergasted by these scenes of normalcy—that people are living their lives as though nothing out of the ordinary is going on, while thousands straggle past them in a tragic caravan, is too preposterous, too insane, to be real. Only the sunflowers seem to notice what's happening; they stand dead in the fields, brown and brittle, row after row after row. The big, spade-shaped leaves on their stalks bend toward each other, nearly clasped together, like hands. Their dark round heads are bowed toward the earth, as if in prayer, or shame.

When the sun shone, the humidity was smothering. When it rained, as it often did, there was no shelter. Farmers burned dead stalks in their fields, filling the air with smoke so sharp that Isadora's eyes brimmed with tears. She had stopped crying over the dead; there were too many to mourn. She was no longer shocked to see soldiers trading the lives of her companions to peasants for money, liquor, or a place to rest for the night. Her mind became as muddy as the road they walked on, filled, it seemed, with thick, brown sludge that little could penetrate. She did what she had to do. She trudged onward.

Occasionally they passed other convoys heading in the opposite direction. Seeing them was one of the few things that still affected her. She thought she knew how bad she felt; she thought she knew how miserable she and her companions looked. But watching the other groups struggle by like tattered zombies, so caked with dirt it looked like they'd clawed themselves from their graves, was like staring into a mirror in which she could see herself and her conditions more clearly. She became saturated with horror, sick with shame, heartbroken for herself. Her one consolation was that she still had her family.

After weeks on the road, the earth ahead opened up like it had been gashed with a giant cleaver. The rolling fields abruptly ended, plummeting down steep cliffs toward a river placidly flowing south. They had reached the Dniester at last. ⌖

EIGHTEEN

Hard figures concerning the numbers of the dead are difficult to ascertain absolutely. The most reputable studies of this period conclude that at the beginning of July 1941, some 190,000 Jews fell under Romanian/German occupation in Bessarabia and Northern Bukovina. Except for 16,000 interned in the ghetto in Chernovitz (the capital of Bukovina), these regions were "cleansed" of every last Jew who had lived there. Though thousands had been killed in massacres before the deportations began, the vast majority were pushed toward the Dniester in convoys like Isadora's. By autumn, some 65,000 Jews, more than one-third of the population just a few months earlier, had died—before ever crossing into Transnistria.

The scenes of carnage that littered the roadsides appalled even the German officers of the SS *Einsatzgruppe D*, the mobile death squad assigned to the area that was, essentially, a Nazi special-forces execution team. They had no complaints about the numbers of Jews killed, but were revolted by Romanian negligence in dealing with the corpses, which were left unburied and would soon become severe biological hazards. Eventually, the Romanians sent a small advance team ahead of each convoy to dig pits every ten kilometers, each of which could hold one hundred bodies. Even these overflowed.

NINETEEN

The road from the plateau down to the Dniester was a ramp of mud as steep as a ski jump. The convoy slowed, not for the people's sake, but so the horses pulling the wagons could keep their footing. Many of the deportees fell, over and over, too weak to resist the pull of gravity on the slick terrain; those with enough life left in them thrashed in the muck while sliding down the hill, trying to get to their feet before being pummeled with rifle butts or lashed with riding crops. Anna, who was in the worst shape of anyone in Isadora's family, emaciated and flirting with delirium, simply couldn't stay upright for more than a few paces at a time. Dutsu tried supporting her, her arm dripping with clay draped over his shoulder and around his neck, but finally concluded that the only way to keep her with them was to physically drag her. He told Vili to take her other arm and, with Anna facing backward, they pulled her along between them, her heels plowing trenches in the mud.

At the bottom of the hill, on the western bank of the Dniester, sat the town of Atachi, or at least what was left of it. At a key position by a bridge that crossed the river, it was hard hit during the Axis advance. Most of the buildings were in shambles, like architectural amputees, missing roofs or walls, charred by fire. The local Jewish population had been exterminated in pogroms, and of the thousands that arrived there on foot, many left only in spirit. Their bodies remained, contorted, partially eaten by dogs and crows, in the streets and along the riverbank. The walls that still stood were covered with desperate graffiti, scribbled in charcoal, which read, YOU WHO COME HERE, SAY KADDISH FOR THE DEAD, or HERE WAS MURDERED ABRAMOWITZ AND ALL HIS FAMILY.

The deportees deposited temporarily in town looked hardly better off than the dead, crowded densely into the ruins. In contrast to the quiet of the convoy, Atachi reverberated with the wails of the sick, the injured, and the mad. Nowhere was there enough space to accommodate Isadora's group; after being led through the streets, their pitiful procession was ordered to a halt under a stand of trees beside the river, with a canopy of leaves turning red and yellow for a roof and soggy earth for a floor. It was better than most of the accommodation they had had along the way, but Isadora was too drained to appreciate it, especially as she was distracted by a scene occurring nearby. Romanian soldiers were entertaining themselves by forcing Jews into the river at gunpoint, taunting their God to repeat the parting of the Red Sea. The first to turn back when the water deepened was shot. The others waded on toward the opposite shore and, too weak to fight the current, were swept downstream. There would be no miracles on this day.

For a couple of days they camped under the trees. Isadora was grateful, mostly because she knew her mother would die soon without a rest. Mitzi persuaded the family to make the best of the moment and have a feast, for who knew what was coming next? Dutsu went into town and returned with a loaf of bread, one hard-boiled egg for each of them, and a small pail of fresh milk, which they consumed all at once. It was more food than any of them had eaten in a single sitting since leaving Balti, and over the next weeks and months, Isadora would return to the memory of that day, especially the taste of the warm, thick milk, which coated her stomach with what felt like love, and gave her the brief sensation of being full.

The following morning, shouts and curses brought Isadora's convoy to its feet, except for those who had died over the previous three nights. Anna had recovered a little of her strength, and needed only a steadying hand to help her to the bridge. They walked across the quarter-mile span, into the city of Moghilev, into Transnistria.

In the year lasting from autumn 1941 to autumn 1942, some 55,000 Jews crossed the Dniester into Moghilev, making it Transnistria's busiest gate of entry. Like Atachi, Moghilev had been virtually destroyed in the fighting between the Axis and Soviet armies, its half-collapsed homes and buildings hardly able to meet the definition of shelter. Deportees—some of whom stayed in Moghilev, most others who paused there temporarily before being marched on to further, more rural destinations— were crammed into bombed-out homes, more than thirty sickly people piled atop each other in a single room. Pigsties and horse stalls were packed with people living in conditions unfit for the animals they were meant to hold.

As a way to reduce pressure on the city and limit the spread of typhus, which swept through the community in epidemic proportions, some of the houses and barns were locked, then set ablaze, incinerating alive hundreds of Jews at a time. Collective graves were filled to capacity with the bodies of those who had died from illness and starvation, or who were machine-gunned by Nazi death squads. Yet by all accounts, it was the lucky ones who were allowed to remain in Moghilev. ❧

TWENTY

Thumbs hitched under the shoulder straps of my backpack, I walked across the bridge, a no-man's-land suspended between borders. Behind me was the Moldovan town of Atachi. Before me hung a blue banner with yellow Cyrillic letters that spelled UKRAINA. Below me flowed the Dniester River, dark green bordering on black, its tranquility broken by faint ripples that snaked around glassy patches on the surface. It was a sunny, early autumn day, the same season, give or take a week or two, as when my grandmother crossed the river sixty-four years earlier. Lining the grassy banks, leafy trees were turning yellow and red. Above them on the Ukrainian side glinted the three silvery onion domes of an Orthodox cathedral. Everything seemed peaceful, pretty. There was no indication, not the faintest sinister aura, of the atrocities that had once occurred there.

I knew nothing but history about Moghilev. Not a word was written about it in my Ukrainian guidebook, leaving me to wonder how challenging it would be to navigate when I only spoke a single phrase in the local language—*harna sobaka*, meaning "good dog." Cardboard crates filled with apples and bananas sat outside the Ukrainian customshouse, stacked on dollies, waiting to pass inspection. Inside the hall lit only with ambient light from the dirty windows, five immigration agents lingered around, looking bored, smoking cigarettes and crushing their butts on the beige tiled floor. A dinosaur of an X-ray machine—both in age and size—sat in the middle of the room.

I was the only person crossing the border at the moment, and was greeted with friendly curiosity by the customs officers, who rarely saw Americans. A moment of excited interest was followed by one of those uncomfortable pauses that sometimes intrude when people on opposite sides of a language barrier first adjust to being in the same room, seeking a balance between recognizing and politely ignoring each other because there's nothing to say—like riding in an elevator with strangers. While the agent at the desk leafed through my passport and looked perplexedly at an old computer monitor, another officer took advantage of the delay to motion me into a back room. I followed.

We stood a few feet in from the doorway, facing each other. He was old, with thin, gray hair and a pale, creased face, and movements like those of a tortoise—intent, but unbelievably slow. Speaking quietly in Ukrainian, he said something I couldn't understand. Repeating himself, he failed to aid my comprehension. His whole demeanor was so sheepish, it wasn't until he tentatively held out his open palm that it became evident he was trying to shake me down. He stood there, his hand wavering, looking at me with sad, imploring eyes. It was an interesting technique—arousing sympathy rather than fear—and I nearly took pity on the man, but not quite; I walked out of the room and left him there, his palm still open. Back in the main hall, the other officers laughed in mockery of what may have been the lamest bribery attempt in the history of this or any other border crossing in the world.

After reclaiming my passport, I was directed into the back room again, this time by a rock of a man in black military pants, combat boots, and a black ribbed sweater with shoulder lapels. He was about half a foot taller than me, broad-chested and thick-armed. He had a crew cut and wore a mustache on his wide Slavic face, along with an impassive expression that conveyed absolute authority. If it was his turn to try to squeeze some money out of me, his methods would surely be different than the old man's.

He sat me down at a table and asked how much money I had. I lied, telling him I traveled with very little cash. Then he wanted to know what kind of valuables I was carrying. There was my camera. How much was it worth? I lied again, cutting its value in half. Our conversation was halting, each word framed by the flipping of phrasebook pages. I was guarded, wondering if he extorted on a sliding scale. But finally, when he started scribbling on a Xeroxed form, I saw that he was just gathering information with which to fill out a customs declaration. I relaxed. When the paperwork was finished, he asked me where I was staying. I said, "A hotel."

"Which hotel?" he wanted to know.

"I don't know," I said. "I'm going to look for one," I explained, pointing to my eyes, then making a walking motion with my fingers like in the old Yellow Pages ads.

He wrote down the names of two hotels on a piece of paper.

"Which is the cheapest one?" I asked.

"The Olympic," he said. Then he stood up and indicated that I should follow him. "My name," he added in English, "is Torik."

As we left the building, Torik grabbed two apples from one of the boxes awaiting inspection and handed them to me. Heading toward the street, I imagined he was going to point me to the hotel. Instead, we crossed the road, entered a restaurant, and walked straight to a private room in the back, just big enough for a long wooden table and a few chairs. A slim young woman followed us in with a small decanter full of vodka and a couple of shot glasses. Torik introduced me to her, then said a few things I didn't understand. The waitress left, Torik poured us each a shot, and we toasted to Ukrainian-American friendship.

Within minutes the waitress was back with a tray full of food—borscht, salad, bread, cheese, and fried liver. Torik, with the insistence of a Jewish mother, urged me to eat, so we ate, and we drank. Once we were sufficiently lubed to make the language barrier seem like a mere hurdle, we talked, gesturing and passing the phrasebook back and forth. Torik revealed that he'd once served proudly in the Soviet army, and was eager to teach me to drink like a Russian soldier. He balanced a shot glass full of vodka on his elbow, then thrust the liquor into his mouth with astonishing precision. He prodded me to try, but I was sure I'd end up showering myself with vodka and chipping a tooth on the glass. Perhaps my lack of manliness inspired him to tell me of a peacekeeping mission upon which he'd served alongside American and French soldiers; the Green Berets and the Foreign Legion were a bunch of wimps compared to the Russians, he pronounced. Vietnam, he continued, was proof the Americans would've been no match for the Red Army. I toyed with reminding him of a place called Afghanistan but, sensing this could be touchy territory, I just shrugged, conveying neither agreement nor protest.

I asked him how old he was, and he said, "Thirty-five."

"Oh, I'm thirty-five, too," I answered.

"You're thirty-five?" he asked, surprised. "Then why are you so small?"

He took off his sweater, pulled up his shirtsleeves, and flexed his biceps. "See," he said, "big!" then reached across the table, squeezed my arms, and shook his head with a pitying smile. He was at once gregarious, magnanimous, and slightly condescending. He would've made the perfect frat boy.

Torik wanted badly to communicate, but even with the vodka, our conversation was stunted. He said his daughter spoke English, and invited me to visit his home later that night. Then he asked me if I liked to shoot guns, saying we could always go somewhere to blast off a few rounds. He gave me his phone number and practically ordered me to call him at 8:30, when he'd be done with work, which he had to be getting back to. We rose to leave, and he dismissed my move to pay for the food. Then he pulled out his cell phone and called me a taxi. When it arrived, he told the driver to take me to the Olympic Hotel and paid the fare in advance, again waving away the cash I tried to hand him. As the cab pulled away from the curb, I smiled and shook my head in wonder at this unexpected welcome into Ukraine.

After checking into the hotel, I checked out the town. It was a small and pleasant backwater, with one main street, shaded residential neighborhoods, and a wooded park that felt creepy after dark. I went back to my room to rest, uncertain whether or not I was going to phone Torik. I was exhausted, having gotten up before dawn to catch a minivan out of Iasi, in Romania, then traveling clear across the nation of Moldova. I'd stopped in Balti, with thoughts of staying there, but the city had become a living museum of postwar Communist architectural weirdness, and after a few hours I conceded that there was no way to get even a remote sense of what it would have been like when my grandmother had lived there. So I'd pressed on to Moghilev. I lay on my bed and closed my eyes, hoping to nap for an hour before 8:30.

At 8:15, I was roused by fists pounding on the door. When I opened it, Torik burst into the room. "Hurry up, let's go, let's go!" he commanded in Ukrainian, in a tone that required no translation and was impossible to defy. He watched impatiently as I gathered a few things, then he whisked me out the hotel door and into the car of his friend and fellow customs officer. From the driver's seat, Vova greeted me with a wide smile, a couple of silver teeth among his white ones gleaming in the light of the streetlamp above us. Speeding off through the streets of Moghilev, I tracked our route, so I'd be able to find my way back without them if I had to.

The car pulled to a stop outside a multistory brick-faced building, and I followed through an open doorway and up a flight of grungy cement stairs. Torik let us into his apartment, which was simple and clean, with faux-finished peach walls that were completely bare but for two hanging strings of plastic chili peppers, one red, the other green. An ochre Oriental-style rug covered the wood floor in the living room; the only piece of furniture was a brown velveteen lounge chair in the corner. A hearty ambrosia of home cooking came from the kitchen, where I met Aliona, Torik's wife, and Victoria, Vova's wife, as well as Torik's daughter, Nastia, who turned out to be ten. I wondered how much English she could possibly speak.

Torik immediately held up for my approval his fluffy orange cat, Lola, then hurled her across the living room. Lola's paws stuck like suction cups to a cushion propped against the wall, and she dropped gracefully to the floor as Torik smiled proudly at her talent. Nastia played with Vova like he was a favorite uncle, running at and jumping on him with delight; something about her laugh, her exuberance, her total lack of defendedness clearly conveyed that this was a well-loved child. And Vova played with her like there was nothing in the world he'd rather be doing. It gave me an instant sense of comfort, which was temporarily disrupted when Torik asked me to follow him. He led me to the bathroom, turned on the tub, and said, "Douche!"

"What?" I answered.

"Douche! Douche!" he ordered, in his preferred style of communicating.

"No, I'm okay," I said. But this was not an offer.

He thrust a towel at me and again said, "Douche—and fast!" End of discussion.

I got in the shower, thinking this was a pretty bizarre way to start an evening, wondering if he thought he was doing me a favor, or if he was trying to get me to do them a favor. Focusing on the latter possibility, I began to feel self-conscious. Was I smelly? Was I dressed inappropriately? When I put my clothes back on, I tried to manipulate my attire so I was as presentable as possible, buttoning my flannel to hide the stains on my T-shirt, and tucking it in. I soon discovered I had nothing to worry about. When Torik came out of the shower himself, he sat down at the dinner table wearing only boxer shorts, his hairy chest completely bare.

Aliona was thirty, with dyed orange hair and a couple of gold teeth. Her bright eyes and charming smile conveyed a genuine inner sweetness. She covered the table with bowls of chicken soup, then platters of stuffed roasted peppers, roasted vegetable salad, sausages, sour cream, and bread. Meanwhile, Torik filled the shot glasses with vodka for the first of countless times. Victoria, gentle and witty, with fair skin and short blonde hair, spoke English well, so became the conduit for conversation as we ate and drank. (Though Nastia was studying English in school, she'd mastered only a few simple phrases.) My mistake was thinking that dinner was to be eaten like at home—all at once—rather than pacing myself to graze all night long. The food wasn't the point at all, really; it was just ballast to support the drinking and the dialogue.

I showed them pictures of my home, pets, and family—a tried-and-true method of bridging a language gap. They showed me pictures from their vacation in Crimea. They wanted to know why, of all possible places, I had come to Moghilev. I paused, unsure of the reactions I'd get when I told them. I wondered, especially, about

Torik's. I tried to imagine what he would have been like, what he would have done, had he lived in Moghilev during the war. With his outsized personality, which embodied both blind nationalistic, military pride, and true kindness, I just as easily pictured him leading a pogrom as risking his neck to save Jews' lives. After my encounter with Gheorgie, I was wary, but in the moment, sitting around a table covered with food and vodka bottles, I felt I could trust my new friends.

I explained, and Victoria translated while the others listened quietly, well aware of what had taken place in their town sixty-odd years earlier. A moment of respectful, perhaps awkward, silence was broken by Torik. "I have one good friend who is Jewish!" he exclaimed, and seemed happy, now, to have a second. When I told them of my plans to travel deeper into Ukraine, to the village where my grandmother had spent a couple of years in a concentration camp, Torik said that if I'd wait a few days, until he and Vova had a day off, they'd drive me there. I was surprised by their generosity, since the town in question was many hours away, but I politely declined. I needed to go there alone, I said. They understood. I began to think that it might have been a good thing for the Jews if Torik had lived in Moghilev during the war. The next round of shots was poured and swallowed, and the conversation shifted to lighter topics.

It seemed like a pretty normal evening, until Nastia was sent to bed and Torik decided to pull out the karaoke machine. To the tunes of popular Ukrainian songs, Cyrillic script popped up on the TV screen, accompanied by images of the Pyramids, the Taj Mahal, and other exotic places. Still in his boxers, Torik slung his arm around me and prodded me to sing a duet with him. We stood side by side, arms over each other's shoulders, him crooning away, full of heart, while I laughed helplessly. He sang a couple of songs, then Vova did a few numbers. When their enthusiasm for their lounge act waned, Torik showed me a home video he'd made on a training trip to Minsk with his coworkers. It was like *Customs Agents Gone Wild*, featuring mostly large, half-naked men getting shit-faced, the floor of their hotel room littered with documents and empty bottles. Torik pointed to the screen and flicked his neck with his middle finger, teaching me the essential Ukrainian gesture, meaning, "to be wasted."

We returned to the table for more booze, and to try on Torik's old Soviet army winter hat, which we passed around, and which he brought out mostly to show how big his head was. By this time, I believe, we were well into our third liter of store-bought vodka. Maybe we'd finished those already and were working on the half-gallon of homemade stuff that Torik had brought out in an old apple juice jar. I'm not sure.

I felt like some unspoken code required me to keep up with my hosts in order to not offend and to earn their respect, and for a while, I was amazed that, shot after shot, I hardly felt more than a little tipsy. But there's always that point when, after ambling around on a happy plateau of moderate drunkenness, you realize you're fast approaching the edge of the cliff of total inebriation. After a couple shots of Torik's moonshine, I was there. *No more*, I thought to myself. I'd rather look weak than prove it by vomiting on the table. But then, a couple minutes after midnight, Victoria announced that it was now nine years to the day since her father had died, and we had to drink in his honor. How can you refuse a toast to a dead man? Luckily, we were required to dribble a bit out of our glasses, onto our plates, in his memory.

Pleading exhaustion, I thanked them all for their hospitality, and said I could walk back to the hotel. I didn't want to trouble them, and would have been grateful for some fresh air. With his usual well-meaning bullishness, Torik insisted on taking me back by car. He threw the trench coat of his customs uniform on over his boxers and, as we headed out into the frigid night, he asked, "In America, do many people drive drunk?"

The next morning, I rose at ten, groggy and drained. Since five, I'd been getting up every hour to go to the bathroom, as though I'd done a vodka cleanse. I headed out of the hotel with no plans beyond finding some coffee with which to screw my head on straight. Just as I reached the bottom of the stairs, Torik appeared.

"Let's go!" he said "Hurry up!" As we walked down the driveway, he opened his black leather vest, revealing the semiautomatic pistol strapped inside.

TWENTY-ONE

The stench of rotting flesh saturated the streets. Sounds of every shade of agony echoed off the walls. Isadora's convoy was marched through the apocalyptic cityscape of Moghilev, and herded directly to its outskirts. Mixed with the relief of being beyond it was the fear that she and her family were headed somewhere even worse, though such a place was impossible to picture. Why, she wondered, with futile intensity for the millionth time, had they ever left Bucharest?

Beyond Moghilev, the convoy climbed out of the river valley. The road was steep, cutting diagonally across the face of a nearly sheer slope; to the right, the cliff rose like a fortress; to the left, it dropped precipitously into a narrow canyon. The dirt track had melted under the rains, and rivulets of runoff poured down the road in turbid, ochre ribbons. Chunks had eroded from the left shoulder and slid off into the gorge. The horses snorted and whinnied, struggling to pull the wagons through the wet clay. People slipped and fell, and found little purchase with which to lever themselves upright. Some were too weak to fight the suction of the mud, and simply toppled forward into it, where they remained like dinosaurs in a tar pit. A few slipped over the edge of the cliff and plummeted to their deaths. Some, naturally, were shot. Most, including Isadora's family, crawled their way forward on their hands and knees, sinking in to their chests. They seemed to be swimming up a river the color and texture of mustard.

By the time they reached the top of the plateau, Isadora's body was plastered with mud and her skinny arms were shaking uncontrollably. Her uncles and her brother were slightly better off, and her aunts were okay, but her mother appeared to be on the verge of irreversible exhaustion—a doomed look Isadora had seen on others countless times before. Fortunately, they were made to move no further that day; the soldiers, tired themselves, had judged that the horses needed a rest.

For the next few weeks, Isadora's convoy shuffled around the roads of Transnistria in a random elliptical route, following arbitrary marching orders with no particular goal except perhaps to see how many people could die before the convoy got to where it was going—if it was going anywhere at all. In many respects, life wasn't much different than it had been before they crossed the Dniester, except that it was rapidly growing worse. Personal property had dwindled, forcing the Jews to stretch even more thinly the food they bought from local peasants. Clothing had shredded, leaving many people half-naked; Isadora's pants were torn and grimy, and her shirtsleeves looked like they'd been flayed by a tiger. Her hair, like everyone else's, was alive with lice. And, as they moved through October and into November, temperatures began to plummet, with the arrival of the coldest winter in a generation.

Sometime after passing through Moghilev, while staggering down the roads to who-knows-where, Anna's legs gave out. Vili and Dutsu tried to lift her up quickly, as they'd done so many times before, but this time she was powerless to help them. Her ankles folded, knees buckled, arms flailed. Her eyes, locked on Dutsu's, conveyed contradictory messages in a single potent glance: *Help me*, and *It's too late.* Isadora looked on, jolted from her habitually disembodied state by the recognition that her mother might have only moments to live. Panic gripped her as she saw her mother sink back to the ground, her scarf-covered head bowed forward. Isa's uncles were too weak to carry her. Others in the convoy straggled past the family as Anna's brothers desperately tried to jump-start her spirit or figure out a way to drag her along.

"Keep up or you'll be shot!" came the cry from a soldier at the back of the line—a cry so familiar it had become dull with repetition. Only this time it was being shouted at *them*, and it rang with the terror of the first time they had ever heard it.

A Romanian soldier strode toward them, rifle in hand, his expression blank. Isadora dropped to her knees and hugged her mother. She didn't care if she got shot along with her; she simply didn't want to leave her there. Yisrael stood over them like a flimsy shield, his back to the approaching soldier. Mitzi stood off to the side, pleading with the children to come to her. But they wouldn't. Really, it all happened so quickly. The soldier, still coming at them, lifted his gun. Dutsu shouted "Wait!" and held up in the air the last most-valuable piece of jewelry that the family owned. "Take this and put her in the wagon—please!" he begged. "She'll be better soon. She just needs to rest."

The soldier paused to examine the gold bracelet, gave a noncommittal nod, and stuffed it in his pocket. Then he raised his rifle swiftly, aimed it at Anna, and, as the pocket of air around them filled with the family's gasps and shrieks, the soldier started laughing and lowered his gun. He waved the wagon to a halt and helped Dutsu lift Anna into the back, where a few near-dead children and adults already lay.

Anna never regained her strength, nor did she die—at least, not yet. She trundled along in the back of the wagon, as most of her original companions expired and were tossed to the ground and new ones took their places. Along the way, her shoes were stolen, maybe by a Ukrainian peasant, perhaps by a desperate Jew. Her exposed feet froze, and gangrene set in.

Blizzards soon swept across the land. Torrents of snow exploded from the sky, the icy flakes flung with such force that they stung the skin like small shards of glass. The convoy straggled on, trapped in a swirling world of white, unable to see more than a few feet in any direction. The wind sliced through the rags they wore, sliced right through their skeletal selves, as though their bodies were made of gauze. Flesh froze, bones felt brittle. Feet, so used to sinking into mud, now plunged into snow. Isadora's toes were bitten hard by frost, losing all feeling, then turning black. Temperatures dove well below zero. Before long, waist-high drifts covered the road; Jewish men were sent to the front of the convoy to break trail. The many feet of those who followed packed down a corridor in the snow, over which only the deportees' torsos and heads were visible. It was the start of an epic winter, the likes of which few local Ukrainians had ever seen themselves; winters like this, many of them thought, only existed in exaggerated tales told by their grandparents.

At last, sometime around the middle of November, the soldiers ordered the convoy to a halt for the last time. They had arrived at the village of Obodovka, much of which had been abandoned, and plenty of which had been damaged as the German and Romanian armies rolled eastward across Transnistria. It looked like a snow-bound ghost town. About ten weeks had passed since Isadora had left Balti and the life she had led there, which now felt gilded with unreality, like something about which she'd once dreamed. ⊙⟨⟩⊱

TWENTY-TWO

Heading out the door of the Olympic Hotel, I had a vague idea what Torik had in mind for us. Feeling wobbly, coffee and food had to come before anything else, including guns. We walked to the center of town for breakfast, and again, Torik refused to let me pay a cent, leaving me to wonder how a Ukrainian government employee could afford to be so magnanimous. My best guess, after having paused on the sidewalk to chat amiably with a couple of dapper older men who Torik described as "big mafia," is that his work as a customs officer probably had a few side benefits.

Before being irresistibly swept up in his agenda, I tried asking if there was a museum in town commemorating the Holocaust in Moghilev, which I'd remembered once hearing something about. Unable to immediately understand what I was saying, Torik rang Victoria on his cell phone, so she could translate for us. When he handed the phone to me, she mentioned that there was going to be a memorial gathering for her father that afternoon, and said that it would make her very happy if I could be there. She suggested that Torik and I visit the museum, which he'd know how to find, then go together to the cemetery. I gave the phone back to Torik so Victoria could explain the plan.

On the way to the Jewish museum, walking along a quiet row of single-story houses with pitched roofs and plain-plastered facades, Torik pointed to one and said it was the local synagogue. At that very moment, two young men emerged from it, dressed in black fedoras, black suits, and black shoes, their cheeks sprouting with the spotty, scraggly beards of twenty-something Lubovitchers. We stopped them and said hello, Torik explaining in Ukrainian that I was of the tribe. They ushered me inside the foyer of the building, while Torik waited outside. One of them, named Chaim, spoke English. After a few pleasantries, he said that that night, there would be services followed by a feast to celebrate the start of Rosh Hashanah, the Jewish New Year. He implored me to come back at six.

Having lost track of the calendar somewhere back in Romania, I had no idea it was Rosh Hashanah. That I was suddenly invited to bring in the new year with the local Jewish community seemed at once like an unbelievable stroke of luck and the perfectly natural convergence of every little thing that had put me on that particular street at that precise moment. The invitation to attend services seemed to come as much from life itself as from Chaim, and I accepted.

The museum was a simple affair—a single room, its blue-tiled walls covered with blurry, black-and-white photographs of Jews who had died in Moghilev during the war. There was a memorial flame of sorts, made of red tissue paper, which glowed and fluttered when the light and fan beneath it were switched on. Behind it was a hand-drawn, poster-board map of Moghilev, with tiny lightbulbs placed at the points where various massacres had occurred. The display would have earned high marks as a middle school history project.

The director, Avram Davidovitch, was an elderly man dressed in a V-neck sweater and a sports coat, with snow-white hair parted to the side and delicate facial features that formed gentle expressions. He spoke a little English, not much, so he phoned a friend to translate between us. Passing the receiver back and forth, I explained that I believed my grandmother had crossed the river at Moghilev with her convoy, en route to the camp at the village of Obodovka, and wondered if they had any records or lists of the Jews who had transited through town. No, Mr. Davidovitch said. So many people had passed through Moghilev, in scenes of such pandemonium, that the only lists they had were of those who died there. It was certainly possible, indeed probable, that she had come this way, he added, even though it would be impossible to document.

I measured virtually everything that my grandparents had told me about their lives against the historical record, to make sure their memories fell within a certain range of accuracy. With memories being what they are, there's no way to determine the veracity of every last recollection, but as long as their stories weren't contradicted by objective facts, I was inclined to believe them. Hearing that it was "possible, indeed probable" that my grandmother had passed through Moghilev was verification enough by these standards. And even if she'd confused the names later in life and crossed the river at another point, say at Iampol, further south (where some who ended up at Obodovka are known to have crossed), I felt that the essence of her story would be unaffected by such a mistake.

Torik and I went back to his apartment for lunch. As soon as we got there, he phoned his one Jewish friend to wish him a happy new year. Aliona dished up leftovers from the night before, and as we sat at the table, Torik refilling his shot glass a few times with moonshine from the apple juice jar, Nastia arrived home from school. She greeted me with glee, and plopped down in the seat next to mine, eager to show me her English books and practice what she was learning. She attached herself to me as though I was the older brother she didn't have. On the way to Victoria's father's memorial, she walked right beside me, taking my hand, advising me to be careful of passing cars. She plucked colorful leaves from trees along the way and presented them to me as gifts. She led the way up the dirt path to the cemetery, thoughtfully holding the branches of bushes so they wouldn't snap back and strike me. (In some ways, she looked out for me like I was the *younger* brother she didn't have.)

The cemetery was terraced into the slope of a hillside, with metal picnic tables interspersed among the headstones in clearings surrounded by thick foliage. Victoria was busy cleaning her father's grave; she lit candles and placed them on the slab, poured a glass of vodka and another of seltzer and set them next to the candles, then put some candy and cheese and meat on a plate, which she laid with care beside the glasses. Meanwhile, two of her aunts spread a cloth over the nearby picnic table, then covered every inch of it with plastic plates heaped with roast duck, salads, smoked fish, sausages, cheeses, fried potatoes, and sliced apples. There were a couple of bottles each of vodka and wine, and, when the aunts announced that everything was ready, cups were raised to honor the dead man before the eating began in earnest.

"My father loved to have people over to the house for meals," Victoria told me, "so sometimes we come here, to his place, to eat with him now." It made perfect sense, and the mood, on this warm, sunny autumn afternoon, was as festive as I imagine Victoria's father would have liked. Funny stories were told about the dead man as the delicacies were devoured with gusto. There were no religious overtones, and not a moment was somber.

Before I knew it, it was 4:30, and I needed to head back to town to get ready for temple. Torik and Nastia came with me. When we reached the hotel gate, we said good-bye, certain we wouldn't see each other again before I left for Obodovka the next day. Torik opened his leather vest, showing me his gun again, and said, "Next time," making shooting motions with his right hand. Nastia leapt forward and gave me a hug, saying, "We will see you again."

"I hope so," I said, knowing it was unlikely. Good-byes like this—sweet, sad, and final—become familiar moments when you travel enough, but that doesn't make them any less affecting. I walked toward the door of the hotel brimming with gratitude for having met them, and feeling a stab of loss at their passing so quickly through my life.

I had one shirt that would pass as clean. As for pants, the best I could do was pick the pair that was less dirty. For shoes, it was either worn-out sandals or mud-stained boots. I was definitely not temple-ready by any American standards; next to the Hasids, I was going to look like a slob. Upon entering the temple, however, any anxieties about my appearance were assuaged as fast as when Torik came to the dinner table in his boxers. Some of the men in the large yellow room were wearing suit jackets, one with a chestful of Soviet army medals. But others sat on benches around a long table in jeans and sweaters. One old man—who looked exactly as I'd imagined the peasants in Sholom Aleichem stories, his expression at once dreamy and world-weary, like at any moment he could just as easily burst into laughter or tears—wore a frayed flannel shirt and torn shoes. His sausage-fingered hands were stained indigo, as though he'd been squeezing blackberries or worked an old printing press for most of his life. Everyone wore a yarmulke. Chaim and his partner were the only two Orthodox Jews; they'd been sent from Israel for the occasion, since Moghilev had no rabbi of its own.

There were about twenty men in all, talking in small clusters or sitting quietly, most of their faces limp, tired. Nearly all of them looked to be over sixty, and many of them seemed familiar. There was a dead ringer for Leonard Nimoy; one looked just like my grandfather Joshua's old friend Seymour, with a shock of frizzy hair and bushy brows sharply arched over beady oval eyes; another had a face more like my mother's father than anyone I'd ever seen. The women, all four of them, of the same generation as the men, sat in a separate room. They'd wait there until the prayers were finished and it was time to serve the food, and didn't seem to mind.

At sunset, services began. Fading golden light filtered through the sheer, lacy curtains covering the windows that faced the street. Some brown bookshelves hung on the walls, with a couple of menorahs atop them. A dark wooden wardrobe served as the Holy Ark. While Chaim led the prayers, his partner coached the congregation as to what they were expected to be doing. It was instantly clear that most of the men had little experience in a temple. They had to be prompted to respond at the appropriate times with *Baruch hu, baruch sh'mo*—among the most basic of lessons when learning how to pray—and were led slowly through the *Shema*, the most important prayer in Judaism, which is only six words long. While Chaim davenned, often facing the wardrobe and mumbling as though talking to himself, a few of the congregants flipped through their prayer books with puzzled expressions, like they were trying to read an instruction manual written in Japanese. Others talked in the background among themselves, completely ignoring what was going on, which made it feel a lot like Hebrew school.

For their entire lives, any of the men at the service who had prayed had done so in Russian, not Hebrew, Chaim explained to me later. "That's no good," he pronounced, his tone implying that Russian prayers wouldn't even make it past God's secretary.

When the service was over, the women brought in heaping platters of food from the other room, then joined the rest of us around the table for dinner. Plates of honey and sliced apples, eaten to symbolize the anticipated sweetness of the new year, were passed around. Bowls of boiled potatoes with garlic and platters of egg salad were set around the table, along with cans of sardines. No soup was served, nor any kind of meat, which kept things kosher. There was also no traditional round *challah*—baked especially for the High Holidays in the shape of a crown, some say, to remind us that God is King of the Universe, or perhaps as a symbol of the cyclical nature of life. And instead of making Kiddush over wine, it was said over vodka shots. I wondered if there was any negotiation on this point between Chaim and the congregants, with the locals conceding to do the entire service in Hebrew and to keep meat off the table, but refusing to budge on the vodka-versus-wine issue.

The men and women bantered familiarly as they ate. Then, as if on cue, everyone promptly got up and left at 7:15. Following their lead, I rose to go and said good-bye to Chaim.

"If we ever meet again," he said, "I hope you'll speak Hebrew by then, because you know, you can't really be a Jew if you don't."

I assured him I would, and wasn't sure which of us believed me less.

Walking back to the hotel, I reflected on the evening. I'd hardly spoken to anyone other than Chaim. The lack of a common language, I guessed, was mostly to blame, but not completely. Few times in any of my travels, even among very foreign cultures, had I been invited to a gathering where I'd remained such an outsider, unable to connect with others though eye contact, hand gestures, tone of voice, and obvious expressions of goodwill. I felt like I'd been tolerated at the *shul*, but that no one had really been open to engaging. Times had definitely changed since the war; the Ukrainians of Moghilev felt more like my people than did my fellow Jews.

TWENTY-THREE

Obodovka had no walls around it, and the newly formed Jewish ghetto wasn't fenced in. But running away was unthinkable. The winter would have been enough to thwart even healthy people, and the deportees weren't. The soldiers didn't have to worry about them wandering far. Nothing had been prepared for their arrival, and just because their long march was over didn't mean they'd be fed, housed, or cared for in any way. Deposited in an abandoned part of the village, the Jews were left to fend completely for themselves, scurrying for the first shelter they could find among the houses, sheds, and barns clustered at the base of a long, low ridge where it flattened into a shallow valley.

Isadora's family occupied a mud-brick shed about the size of a king-sized bed. The door was broken in half and the roof—made of straw—had fallen in. Though they were exposed to the sky, they were able to spread the straw over the snow-covered floor, giving them something soft and relatively warm to lie on. They still had the down comforter they'd carried from Balti, and the entire family huddled under it together; in the mornings, when they woke up, they often had to shake off the snow that had fallen during the night.

Isadora's uncles and brother scavenged for food, but found none. Anything that might have been left in the fields or gardens around the village was buried deep beneath the drifts. But they did rustle up a stray cooking pot. Mitzi cleared a corner for a kitchen, where they built small fires, melted snow into drinking water, and cooked the only thing on hand to eat—straw. For months, this would be the staple of their diet, and for the first few weeks was their sole source of sustenance.

They were all weak, starving, and cold when they arrived. Within days of reaching Obodovka, Isadora was stricken with typhus. There was no hospital for her to go to, no medicine for her to take. Her fevered body ached as though its every bone was slowly breaking. She couldn't stop shivering, and burgundy spots speckled her skin. A little relief finally came when she slipped into a state of semiconscious delirium, which is how she remained for the next three weeks. She ate nothing. Anna, crippled by the gangrene that had consumed her feet and was now devouring her legs, lay beside Isadora, keeping her daughter alive by squeezing water from a rag into her mouth, one drop at a time. No one expected her to recover, she seemed so much closer to death than to life.

Then, one night, the fever broke. Isadora awoke, famished, hungrier than she'd ever been in her life; hungry, she says, like an animal. When she speaks of this moment now, she says she understands how the people in the Donner Party could have resorted to cannibalism. She *had* to eat something. She struggled to her feet, and realized she didn't have any shoes on. Somehow she remembered that a mismatched pair of galoshes—one man's and one woman's—had been left in the shed. She found them, but they were much too big, so she stuffed them with straw, put them on, and went out the door into the frozen darkness while her family slept.

She had no idea what she was doing or where she was going. She stumbled through the snow, seeing nothing but imaginary stars that swirled before her eyes like a cloud of electric dust. The next thing she knew, she was standing outside the house of a Ukrainian peasant. She doesn't know how she got there; her family's shed wasn't anywhere near the homes of any local people, and she had never visited any. Her only explanation is that an angel must have lifted her up, carried her though the air, and left her at the peasant's door.

The soft light of a kerosene lamp filtered through the window. She knocked on the door and waited. A man stuck his head out of the house and saw Isadora standing there. His eyes widened at the sight of the pale phantom on his porch.

"Please . . . ," Isadora whispered in Russian.

"Go around to the back," the man said brusquely, scanning the night for any possible witnesses.

Isadora went behind the house. After a few minutes, the man opened a window, thrust some things into her arms, and said, "Now get away from here."

She'd been given a loaf of black bread, two onions, and a chunk of lard the size of a softball. She tore into the bread, hardly chewing before gulping each mouthful down. She devoured one of the onions, not bothering to skin it, and desperately bit into the greasy pig fat. She easily could have consumed three times what she'd been given, but all at once, she stopped eating. She'd remembered her family, and couldn't bring herself to finish the food without sharing it with them. She clutched what was left close to her body, took a few steps, and the world again became a starry dream. She doesn't remember walking back, and doesn't know how she found her way. The angel, she thinks, must have lifted her up once more and then set her down at the threshold of her family's little shed.

Someone in the convoy told an SS officer that Isadora wasn't what she appeared to be. She'd maintained her persona as a boy as well as she could throughout the two-and-a-half-month-long march, even as her clothing tore and her hair began to grow back. She was so emaciated as to be sexless, yet it was impossible to completely hide her identity from the other Jews. The soldiers took so little notice of individual deportees, even when shooting them, that they'd been easy to deceive. When Isadora was ratted out, the German officer went to investigate. It was only days after she'd awoken from the stupor of her illness.

Anna and Isa were the only ones in the shed at the time; Dutsu, Vili, and Sami had been among the able-bodied men rounded up that morning by the soldiers to perform one form or another of menial labor; Yisrael was hiding somewhere to avoid being drafted into a work crew; Renee and Mitzi were scouting around for food. Anna saw the soldier coming from a distance, through the broken door. She urgently ordered Isa to get behind her and crawl under the hay covering the floor, just in case. Anna maneuvered herself so she sat atop her daughter, and waited to find out what the German wanted. He marched in with an air of indignant authority.

"Where is your daughter?" he demanded. Anna plainly didn't understand. The solider tried again, in French.

"I have no daughter," Anna answered.

"Don't lie to me!" the German seethed. "I know you have a daughter. Where is she?"

"I have two sons!" Anna insisted. "And they were both taken away to work this morning!"

Isadora heard the impact of the soldier's boot on her mother's face, followed by Anna's whimpering. She felt the pressure of her mother's body shift atop the straw as it fell to the side. Isadora, however, remained fully concealed.

"Now tell me," the soldier said. "I'd like to meet her."

"I told you," Anna murmured.

The German lunged forward and set upon the rag doll of a woman that lay before him. He yanked her up by her hair with such violence that clumps of it were torn from her scalp, then beat her to the brink of death. She never betrayed her daughter. Isadora kept herself hidden long after the shed grew quiet. When she emerged from the straw, she found her mother a bruised and bloody mess, her nose broken, most of her teeth knocked out, raw bald patches on her head.

Anna did regain consciousness, but never recovered. In the weeks that Isadora had been sick, Anna's gangrene had spread like fungus. Her legs had rotted, turning black and oozing pus, as chunks of flesh fell away to reveal the bone beneath. They reeked with the putrid odor of infection, which filled the shed like a noxious gas. She had also come down with dysentery. Isa and Mitzi swabbed her with the few spare rags they had, but despite their efforts to keep her clean, Anna lay coated in excrement and the fluids that seeped from her wounds.

Anna knew she was going to die. Before she lost consciousness for the last time, she told Isadora to always take care of Yisrael, and to be as good of a person as she could be, no matter what happened in the future. Isadora, who had seen enough people die to know what was going on, curled up next to her mother, held her, and cried.

For days, Anna's corpse lay in the shed. The earth was frozen solid, making it impossible to dig any graves, and Isadora's uncles couldn't bring themselves to pitch their sister's body out like a piece of garbage. They waited for the so-called burial committee to remove her; with no other recourse, the pallbearers dragged Anna's body to the edge of the village and tossed it atop the growing mountain of human carcasses, from which packs of dogs fed. So many deportees were dying so quickly, and so few men were healthy enough to dispose of them, that corpses piled up in the streets by the hundreds, frozen in twisted poses. To walk through the ghetto meant navigating a grotesque obstacle course.

Before long, Renee, Vili, and Yisrael all came down with typhus and dysentery. For the next few weeks, while Dutsu and Sami were out during the day, slaving for the German and Romanian soldiers, Mitzi and Isa nursed the sick, keeping their semi-comatose kin as comfortable as possible. Isadora could practically feel the germs floating like a mist in the shed. Remembering her mother's dying request, Isa tended religiously to Yisrael. She needed him to live. And at last, he began to recover.

Renee and Vili didn't. They died within a couple of days of each other, and their bodies were thrown on a random stack of the dead.

TWENTY-FOUR

By January 1942, the ghetto in Obodovka was encircled with barbed wire, and guards were posted around the perimeter. The fence wasn't erected to imprison the Jews per se, but to contain the typhus epidemic, which had gone wild. No one was allowed in or out. As the winter wore on, the ghetto became a sanitary catastrophe, fueling the inferno of disease, as corpses, garbage, and feces filled not only the streets, but also the houses, stables, and pigsties in which the living, the dying, and the dead were crammed together.

The decimation wreaked by the typhus plague was no secret to the government in Bucharest. Not long before the fence went up around Obodovka, the governor of Transnistria suggested to Antonescu that 85,000 Jews in southern Transnistria be deloused. Antonescu responded, "Let them die." As the catastrophic proportion of the tragedy in Transnistria became apparent, Antonescu remained unrepentant and unmoved. He blamed Jews for everything that was wrong with Romania, from the poverty of its citizens to its absence from the ranks of great nations. The Jews, Antonescu wrote, "have no right to appeal to humanitarian principles. They are getting what's coming to them."

Typhus, in fact, was seen by the authorities as the most efficient means to eliminate the Jews once and for all. The epidemic was so ruthless, spreading death with such speed, that the Nazi advisor for Jewish Affairs assigned to Romania, Gustav Richter, reported to his supervisor in Berlin, Joseph Goebbels: "As far as the Jewish question is concerned, it can now be determined that a man like Antonescu is pursuing much more radical policies in this area than we have done so far."

Over the winter of 1941–42, some 50,000 Jews perished from typhus in Transnistria. More than half of those deaths occurred in the Balta district, where Obodovka was located. By the spring of 1942, 90 percent of the deportees sent to Obodovka had died of a combination of disease, exposure, and starvation.

TWENTY-FIVE

With the arrival of spring, warmer weather came to Obodovka like a liberating hero, forcing the cold that had besieged the village into retreat. The sun shone, snows melted, and trees began to bloom. As the world awoke from a gloomy frozen nightmare, small sparks of hope rekindled in the hearts of the exiles, though their circumstances remained dire.

The quarantine of the ghetto was lifted, since the epidemic had burned itself down to a simmer. Deportees of all ages and genders, still feeble from the ravages of winter, were regularly rounded up by soldiers, set to strenuous labor in the forests and fields, or to digging huge pits in which to bury the multitude of thawing corpses. Many were worked into their own graves. Local peasants hired Jews to till their farmlands, do laundry, and perform other menial tasks, paying a token fee for these services to the soldiers and giving just a few morsels of food to the laborers. Sami and Dutsu counted among the more able-bodied in the ghetto — though in normal circumstances they wouldn't be considered fit for anything — and were often taken by the soldiers, leaving Mitzi to hire herself out to peasants to earn a little bread for the family. Isadora and Yisrael perfected the art of hiding during the roundups, and spent much of their days scavenging for food, of which there still was never enough.

The remnants of the Jewish community organized themselves into various committees. An outdoor soup kitchen was created, providing a small serving of watery gruel to each person on a daily basis. Sanitation crews gradually cleaned the streets, bringing them to an acceptable level of filth. A small police force kept order, especially as new deportees arrived with the resumption of convoys that brought the last of the Jews out of Bessarabia and Bukovina. Makeshift hospitals were established, though in reality they were simply isolation units for those stricken with typhus, not clinics offering treatment, and those who entered rarely emerged alive. Minyans gathered and religious services were held, even though most who had endured the winter had been completely stripped of their faith.

Sami and Dutsu were worked by the soldiers until they were nearly broken. Neither felt that their gaunt bodies could take much more punishment, and they began to speak of escaping into Russian-held territory. They weighed the pros and cons of the idea with Mitzi, as Isadora and Yisrael listened. Though getting out of Obodovka itself wouldn't be difficult, it was surrounded by hostile terrain. If they ran into German or Romanian soldiers, they'd be shot on sight, and the Ukrainians couldn't be trusted to protect them. They had hundreds of miles to travel before they'd reach safety, little strength with which to make the journey, and nothing left with which to bribe people or barter for goods. Successfully escaping with the whole family would have been virtually impossible; their chances of surviving would be poor enough if they went alone, but better, they felt, than if they stayed.

The biggest dilemma they grappled with was the ethical one. They felt like they'd be abandoning their family, to whom they felt duty-bound. But as they talked about it, Mitzi commented that Sami and Dutsu weren't actually doing anything to help the family survive; they provided nothing in the way of food while they shared in eating what Mitzi earned and Isa and Yisrael found. If one of them fell ill, neither Sami nor Dutsu would be able to cure them. If a soldier had a murderous whim and Mitzi, Isa, or Yisrael were in the wrong place at the wrong time, neither Sami nor Dutsu would be able to protect them.

Isadora was torn as she listened to the conversation. She didn't want her uncles to die, but she also didn't want them to leave. While Mitzi may have been right—they weren't actually providing for the family—nevertheless, their presence was a precious comfort in a cruel place.

One night, Sami and Dutsu said good-bye, snuck out of the ghetto, and slipped into the Ukrainian countryside. It would be years before Isadora would learn anything of their fate. Left alone with her sister's two children, Mitzi cared for them as though they were her own.

As spring progressed, a legion of Romanian Orthodox priests descended upon Transnistria. They filled roles as military chaplains and as pastors to Ukrainian communities, who rejoiced at the return of religious life after years of state-imposed atheism under the Soviet regime, when churches were destroyed and local priests were murdered or exiled. Churches were rebuilt across the region; icons were exhumed from hiding to hang proudly once more in people's homes; children were baptized by the thousands; weddings and funerals again became spiritual celebrations rather than bureaucratic chores.

The Romanian Orthodox leadership viewed the war against the Soviets as a battle between God and Satan, in which "the armies of Jesus would destroy the Bolsheviks and their henchmen." Since *Bolshevik* and *Jew* were synonymous in the minds of many Romanians, few priests raised their voices against the subhuman treatment of the deportees. Those who had filtered into the region during the previous fall and winter, witnessing firsthand the worst of the typhus epidemic as well as cold-blooded acts of murder, either ignored the atrocities or hailed them as proof that God truly was on the side of the Romanians. Fortunately, the priest who arrived in Obodovka was of a more compassionate nature; and in one of those rare flashes of luck that seem more at home in works of fiction than in real life, Mitzi recognized him instantly. They had been classmates and friends in high school. The priest also recognized Mitzi. He was cool to her on the street when they first met, for the sake of appearances, but quietly said, "Come find me at the church."

Mitzi went. The priest embraced her, saying how sorry he was to find her there and how glad he was that she was still alive. He listened intently as Mitzi described all that had happened to her family since the invasion of Bessarabia. The priest offered more than a sympathetic ear, assuring Mitzi that he could not only get word of her situation to her fiancé, who had been in Timisoara at the time of the invasion, but also smuggle small items from him to her.

Within a month, the first of several packages arrived from Romania: a few hardcover books, inside the pages of which were tucked modest amounts of cash, which Mitzi easily converted into food. She spent frugally, buying just enough to subsist—in part because she never knew if more would follow, but also to attract as little attention as possible to the fact that she had some money. The books themselves were as joyfully received as the cash hidden within. In the same way that they conserved their money, Isadora rationed her reading, savoring every moment that she was able to escape from Obodovka into the worlds the novels created in her mind. Once she, her brother, and her aunt had all finished a book, Yisrael would rent it out to other deportees, charging a potato, an onion, or half a loaf of bread per week. Despite the scarcity of food, many gladly paid the price, desperate for literary therapy.

Meanwhile, the priest, who always knew when the labor round-ups would take place, warned Mitzi in advance, and she would send Isadora and Yisrael to hide in the church, where they spent hours sheltered in safety. To this day, my grandmother says, thanks to that priest, she's spent more time in churches than in synagogues. While hiding there, the priest schooled Yisrael in the duties of an altar boy. He was shown how to hold the cross, swing a censer, and carry candles, while wearing an ankle-length cassock. Once he'd mastered the rites, Yisrael was summoned for the funerals of soldiers and local people. After the church service, he'd join the procession to the cemetery, marching at the back of the line, carrying one of the plates of food brought by the mourners for the post-burial feast— perhaps a cake or a slab of ham. When no one was looking, he'd dart down an alley or behind a house, stay out of sight for a few minutes, then go back to the church, where he'd leave the robe before carrying his prize back to his sister and aunt.

Over the summer, for the first time in a year, Isadora felt like she had a slight edge over death. She was still hungry most of the time, but she could feel her body responding to the slight increase in its intake. Meanwhile, she made her first real friends in the ghetto. Renee Ghinsberg was a petite seventeen-year-old girl, with dark hair and eyes, and the wearied expression of someone who'd endured more sadness than could be digested over too short a time. On the eve of Operation Barbarossa, she'd been living with her mother, who was a dentist, and her father, who was a wealthy grain merchant, in the Bessarabian city of Secureni. Along with her mother's dental assistant, a young man named Martin Wexer, and thousands of others, the family had been deported. Theirs was one of the earliest convoys, among those marched across the Dniester only to be repelled back over the river by German forces. For about a month, they were held on the Bessarabian side, in the Vertujeni transit camp, along with about 23,000 other Jews.

Each building there was meant to house seventy people, yet every one was packed with upward of five hundred. Water was contaminated, and there were so few wells that Renee had to wait in line for many hours to draw a single bucket. What scant food existed was hardly edible. Hundreds died daily. The Romanian commander of the camp, a decent man who quickly resigned his commission, was aghast at the abominable conditions. He later described a "horrific concentration of . . . women, children, young girls, men, the sick, those who were dying, and women in labor—all having no way to feed themselves . . . They were covered with lice and abscesses, so worn out that . . . some died, others fainted, and pregnant women gave birth . . . Just to see them produced such a state of tension that I could neither eat nor sleep." And once this compassionate commander was replaced by another, more cold-blooded master, things only got worse.

Rape and murder were daily diversions for the camp captains. The deportees were ordered to pave the streets of the camp, but were given no materials to perform the job—a proposition that proved more difficult than making bricks without straw. As weak as they were, they trudged a mile or so to the banks of the Dniester, from where they hauled huge stones back to Vertujeni, afraid to even pause for breath along the way, as those who did were beaten unconscious.

Around the end of August or beginning of September, 1941, Renee's family was herded out of the camp in a convoy with about 3,000 others. They marched through the Cosauti Forest, where, before the technique became notorious at Auschwitz, some of the deportees were ordered to go to the right, and others to the left. Those sent to the left were executed on the spot, while those sent to the right were prodded on to cross the Dniester at Iampol. After many weeks of wandering the frozen Transnistrian roads, much as Isadora had, Renee's convoy was deposited at an abandoned Soviet collective farm, called Dubina, just a few miles from Obodovka. There they wintered in open-sided stables, sleeping on straw, bodies pressed against bodies, while rats scampered over their heads. Renee, her mother, and Martin each came down with typhus, but survived. Her father never caught the disease; while bargaining with a Ukrainian for a loaf of bread, the peasant shot him dead and took the gold coins he held in his hand.

In the spring, Renee, her mother, and Martin were relocated to Obodovka, where at least the houses had walls. After finding a decaying two-room house, empty because all of the deportees who'd occupied it had died, Renee's family moved in and her mother opened a makeshift dental practice for soldiers and Ukrainian peasants. Patients paid with potatoes, flour, and sometimes bacon; in Transnistria, the laws of *kashrut* were laughably irrelevant. Martin met a deportee who'd been a master jeweler; he taught Martin how to fashion false teeth from gold (supplied by the patients) even without any of the proper instruments. Renee spent her time inventing new ways to stretch into meals the small amounts of food her mother and Martin earned. She dreamed of sitting atop a traditional mud-brick oven, feeling its warmth spread through her body, while surrounded by piles of white bread and eating loaf after loaf after loaf.

Neither Renee nor Isadora can recall exactly how they met, but they became fast friends. When she wasn't hiding in the church, Isadora could often be found at Renee's house, where the two would talk for hours, since there was nothing else to do. Soon, they befriended a young man a little older than themselves, named Immanuel Weissglass, whom everyone called "Onu." He had curly golden hair, and his face, despite its thinness, retained an angelic quality. Onu was different from everyone else in the ghetto. He wrote poetry, and, as though he was living in an alternate universe, spoke of life with a romanticism that was at once uplifting and absurd.

Renee quickly developed a crush on him, but Onu only had eyes for Isadora, whose hair had grown out and was pulled back in a pair of blonde braids. Isa was fond of him too, but immune to a full-blown infatuation; she was all too aware of the reality of their circumstances, and thought it a little bit crazy that anyone could think about love or write about beauty in a hellhole like Obodovka. There was no tension in this teenage triangle of unrequited affection; the girls, at least, knew that nothing would ever really come of it, and didn't let it intrude on their friendship. The three of them needed each other's company, which was too precious to spoil with pettiness.

The leaves began to turn and the nights' frigid winds whispered hints of the winter to come. Despite the precautions Mitzi and the priest took to keep their friendship secret, the ghetto had some of the essential characteristics of any small village: People nosed into other people's business, rumors spread with varying degrees of accuracy, and not everyone got along. One of the deportees, my grandmother says, grew jealous that her family had been able to obtain extra food and revealed the alliance between her aunt and the priest to the Romanian soldiers.

Of course it was illegal for the priest to help Isadora's family, but he was far from the only one smuggling goods into Obodovka. Romanian authorities and soldiers in Transnistria had established a profitable underground network which carried care packages to some Jews from relatives they had back in Romania. Transnistrian officials also worked out deals to transport aid from Jewish organizations, which were frantic to assist the deportees yet forbidden from doing so by Antonescu. From the time the money or clothing left the hands of the donors to the time it reached the deportees, about 90 percent of it trickled away down numerous crooked channels. The real crime Mitzi and the priest committed was to circumvent the authorized contraband pipelines, effectively cutting out the graft-hungry officials.

Upon the discovery of their smuggling operation, Mitzi and the priest were arrested, taken away one autumn day without warning. It would be years before Isadora would discover what had happened to them. She assumed her aunt had been shot. Though her mother had died some nine months earlier, this was the first time Isadora truly felt like an orphan.

Isadora and Yisrael were taken in by a family named Parnas, with whom Mitzi had been friends back in Balti. They lived in a wooden barn the size of a two-car garage. The father, balding and bearded, with wire-rimmed spectacles, was a doctor. He did his best to ease the suffering of the sick in Obodovka, despite a complete lack of medicine, and the knowledge that he probably wouldn't save a single life. The mother was kind, and treated Isadora and Yisrael almost as if they were her own, but she was feeble, and Isa took more care of her—and her two children—than she did of Isa. Yisrael helped out by using his well-honed wiles to contribute to the family's food supply. The two of them slept in an old wardrobe that they laid down on the floor, with a few inches of straw for a mattress. They were grateful to have a home, though their hearts were shrouded in a fog of loss too heavy to lift.

As winter set in, times again grew tougher. Food became harder to find, and increasing numbers of Jews in Obodovka starved to death. The typhus epidemic reignited, and hundreds succumbed to it. There was no escape from the cold; even indoors, Isa could see her breath. But it wasn't quite as bad as the previous winter. The Jews had had all summer to prepare for it, rather than arriving with nothing, to nothing, after marching for months on end. Contraband goods from Romania continued to dribble into the village, creating a small but vital black-market economy. The weakest had already been winnowed from the population. And this season, while brutal, failed to reach the record-breaking extremes of the previous year.

Isadora found the darkness most distressing. Her world was once again one of icy gloom, and as the amount of daylight decreased, her hopes of returning to a normal life faded along with it. The winter brought back blizzards of memories from that of the year before, with the anniversaries of the horrible deaths of her mother, her uncle, and her aunt, of losing her toes to the frost, of starving and eating straw, of the endless marching with the convoy, of so many dead. Distracting herself with chores for the Parnas family, sustained by her few cherished friends, Isadora made it through to spring.

TWENTY-SIX

Further east, through the heart of the winter of 1942–43, the Battle of Stalingrad was being waged like the military equivalent of a winner-take-all poker game between Hitler and Stalin, in which each kept raising the stakes, with neither willing to fold. Both believed that this city on the Volga was the keystone to the eastern front, and that if it fell, so would the rest of the Soviet Union. By the time the Axis armies finally surrendered on February 2, 1943—against Hitler's orders—Stalingrad had become the bloodiest battle in human history, with over a million and a half soldiers and civilians dead or wounded. Among them were some 155,000 Romanian troops, or about half of its active field divisions. The Hungarians lost over 130,000 soldiers, and its Second Army was destroyed.

With the successful Soviet defense of the city and their subsequent advance westward, the leaders of the countries aligned with Germany made quick political calculations. They couldn't break their alliances with Germany, and held out hope that Germany might still win the war; but they believed that if the Germans lost, their countries would be judged by the Allies, above all else, by the way they had treated the Jews.

Suddenly, those in Romania who had proposed radical solutions to the Jewish Question voiced moderation. Antonescu's plans to ship to Polish concentration camps some 300,000 Romanian Jews living in the regions of Regat, Transylvania, and the Banat—very few of whom had been deported thus far—were canceled. The government slowly began to allow the Red Cross and Jewish organizations to deliver modest amounts of aid to Transnistria (though none of it reached Obodovka). Meanwhile, Antonescu listened more seriously to pleas to repatriate the Transnistrian deportees, beginning with the orphaned children, and began negotiating with Zionist groups over the logistics of sending Romanian Jews to Palestine. These moves were made solely in order to appear innocent before the world of any crimes against humanity.

Hungary, which after the early massacre at Kamenetz-Podolsk had steadfastly resisted Hitler's demands for a universal deportation of its Jewish population, saw even less reason to comply after Stalingrad, despite increasingly intense Nazi pressure. Following the cataclysmic loss along the Volga, the Hungarian government moved to rectify the most serious abuses inflicted upon the country's Jews by trying to improve the degrading conditions of those drafted into the Hungarian army's labor corps. For my grandfather, this decision came just in time.

TWENTY-SEVEN

Joshua graduated from his high school in Uzhgorod in the spring of 1941 with limited options. Since Jews were forbidden from enrolling in universities, his lifelong dream of becoming a veterinarian would remain just that. Of the two career tracks open to him—becoming a rabbi or a tradesman—the choice was easy. In the fall, he enrolled in a vocational school in Budapest, where he apprenticed under a furniture maker who was the friend of a cousin.

For a year and a half, he learned to work wood on the floor of a large warehouse, carving, sawing, sanding, joining, nailing, finishing, and designing everything from cabinets to chairs to bed frames. Upon completing his studies, he took the licensing exam required by the Cabinetmakers' Guild, as did all of his graduating classmates. When the results were posted, Joshua scanned the list, found his name, and was gratified to see that he'd earned a journeyman's certificate. He took a second look at the list, to see how his friends had done, and noticed something odd: no other Jew in his class had passed the test. He had no doubt that he owed his success to his Hungarian surname.

Joshua returned to Uzhgorod in the summer of 1943, and took a job in a furniture factory owned by one of Bela's friends. He was now the sole supporter of his family, since the straw man to whom Bela had sold his printing business had been pressured by Hungarian authorities to fire Bela and give his job to an unemployed Gentile. Bela absorbed this setback with dignity, using the extra time he now had to concentrate on writing a book about his travels to Palestine. Berta accepted their slide toward poverty with her usual stoicism. She had faith that Bela would find a creative solution to their difficulties and she valued his literary efforts, while being proud of her son for stepping in and providing for the family. And things weren't that bad yet; they ate meat only on Shabbat, but never went hungry; they lived with less, but had just enough. Besides, since Stalingrad, all the talk had changed from *if* Germany might lose the war to *when* it would. It wouldn't last forever, Berta began to sense, and before long they'd be flourishing in Palestine. This was just a bump on the way there.

Aviva, face framed by a pair of shoulder-length brown braids, was now ten. Mischievous and imaginative, there was also a side to her that was surprisingly mature for a girl so young. Though at the dinner table she might mockingly quip Yiddishisms she'd overheard— like, "When you lack butter for the bread, it is not yet poverty" or "Poverty is no disgrace . . . but also no great honor"—she actually complained little. She went to school, played with her friends, and remained an energetic, happy presence around the house.

Joshua worked six days a week, throwing himself into it with gusto. Aside from simply enjoying what he did, focusing on his work kept him from thinking too much about the fact that soon, barring a military miracle by the Russians, he'd be drafted into the Hungarian army's Jewish slave labor corps.

There was no miracle. In September 1943, Joshua was ordered to report for duty at Puspokladany, about one hundred miles south of Uzhgorod.

Bela Szereny (the author's great-grandfather) as a child, with his mother and grandmother, taken in the mid-1890s

Aviva Szereny, Joshua's sister, pictured shortly before being deported to Auschwitz

Bela and his WWI telegraph unit, taken around 1916

*Berta Szereny, Joshua's mother,
taken around 1920*

*Bela in uniform during
WWI, taken around 1916*

Joshua Szereny, taken around 1929

Bela on oars, Joshua in the bow, Berta in the stern of rowboat
on River Uzh, taken 1930 or 1931

Joshua and his mother,
Berta, 1936

Joshua and his sister Aviva,
1936 or 1937

Isadora's parents, Carol and Anna Rosen,
taken around 1921 or 1922

Isadora and her
brother Yisrael,
taken around 1934,
when they lived
in Bucharest

Isadora and her aunt Mitzi a year before they were
deported to Transnistria

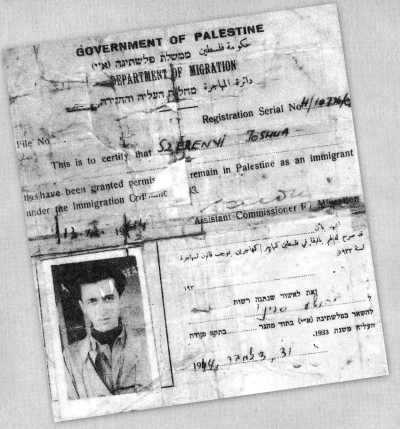

Registration Serial No. H/10776/6

File No.

This is to certify that SZERENYI JOSHUA

has/have been granted permis... ...remain in Palestine as an immigrant
under the Immigration Ord.... ...33.

Assistant Commissioner f.. ..igration

*Joshua's immigration card entitling him to reside in
Palestine, issued December 1944*

*Joshua's high school
photo, 1939*

Bela, Berta, and Aviva Szereny on the streets of Uzhgorod, 1936

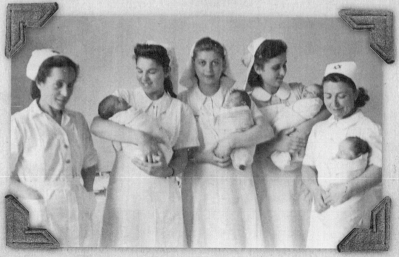

Isadora, in middle, as a delivery room nurse at Hadassah Hospital, Tel Aviv, 1945

Joshua, Isadora, and their first son, Gidon, around 1948

Isadora in Israel, around 1951

The labor units were created in July 1939, initially intended as a form of military service for "unreliable elements" of Hungarian society, including Communists and foreign nationals. Those the army didn't trust with guns—but didn't want to exempt from duty altogether—were given picks and shovels instead. At first, conditions in the labor units were quite tolerable, since they were viewed as an alternative, and honorable, form of service. Before long, however, these units would become the most dreaded instrument in the persecution of Hungarian Jewry.

Within months of Hungary's entry into World War II, uniforms and boots, which had been standard issue, were no longer supplied to Jewish laborers, since German officers couldn't bear the sight of Jews in uniform; instead, they were given caps and yellow armbands to wear with their civilian clothes. When their clothing wore out, the army refused to replace it, making the Jews responsible for dressing themselves while hundreds of miles from home in a war zone. Many were reduced to wearing rags in the midst of the Russian winter. Jewish food rations were stolen by Hungarian officers and replaced with scraps of bones and rotting vegetables. With meager fuel for the Herculean toil into which they were enslaved, malnutrition and disease swelled in the ranks.

Those commanded to build roads and fortifications, as their bodies eroded, and maybe broke, were the lucky ones. On the Ukrainian front, Jews were forced at gunpoint to march across minefields ahead of Hungarian combat units; many thousands of these human minesweepers were blown up in the process, and those who weren't were easy targets for Russian rifles. Other laborers were hitched to wagons and carts, replacing horses that had died of exhaustion. A few commanders ordered their officers to bring no

Jews back alive, prompting the deliberate slaughter of entire units. With no real oversight of the divisions on the front, guards and officers invented a number of popular games, such as the "lakeside vision," in which laborers were taken to muddy bogs and made to somersault through them. In a wintertime favorite, the Hungarians would hose a Jew with water until he became an ice statue. And no laborer wanted to be invited to join the officers for "five o'clock tea"—code for a brutal gang beating.

As time passed and the emaciated, lice-ridden Jewish workers contracted typhus, Hungarian officers, none of whom were doctors, created their own cures. The sick (and sometimes the healthy) were forced to run for fifteen minutes, then jump into an icy river, then stand on the banks to be dried by the frigid wind. In at least one case, guards locked eight hundred ill laborers in a barn, set it on fire and, as the blaze burned down, were pleased to announce that the workers were no longer sick.

Hungarian general Vilmos Nagy, who became defense minister in September 1942, was appalled at the sadistic handling of Jews. Partly from humanitarian motives, and partly from the pragmatic recognition that the army would get better work from well-treated laborers, he ordered rations to be fortified, sick workers to be given leave, and all forms of corporal punishment and physical abuse outlawed. While these orders alleviated the sufferings of the Jews stationed in Hungary proper, commanders on the distant Russian front completely ignored them, even after Stalingrad.

When Joshua received his draft notice, there was good cause for concern. Aside from the torment he might experience at the hands of his own army, the labor corps serving at the front also had to contend with the advancing Soviet forces. Tens of thousands of Jews had died in combat, and tens of thousands more had been taken as prisoners of war. When he boarded the train to Puspokladany, suitcase in hand, sturdy leather boots on his feet, it was the only time he'd ever seen his mother cry.

Upon arriving at the administrative center and processing his paperwork, Joshua was given a yellow armband, an army cap, and an ID booklet marked on the front with a large zs (for *Zsido*, which means "Jew" in Hungarian). He was relieved to learn that he'd been assigned to a unit—Stroma 6/1—that was stationed in Hungary.

Ordered to Szentkiralyszabadja, a small town near Veszprem, he went west by train. He didn't really know what to expect, so wavered between anxiety and calm, depending on what he was imagining at any given moment. "Of course I was nervous," my grandfather remembered, "but what good does that do? The best thing was to be strong, or pretend to be. I calculated that if I stayed in Hungary, and wasn't transferred east, I'd have a pretty good chance of staying alive until the Russians forced Germany to surrender. And when it came down to it, I knew that was the only thing that mattered. I'd heard the terrible stories, and just wanted to live to see my family again. Mostly, though, I tried to forget where I was going, to watch the countryside roll past the windows, to joke around with a few other guys who'd just been assigned to the same unit, to think of nothing."

Arriving at the camp, Joshua was impressed at once by its size. Some 5,000 forced laborers were based there; many were Jews, but there were also units of Yugoslav and Romanian nationals. Their collective mission was to build a military airfield just a few miles north of Lake Balaton in an area surrounded by plowed fields and patches of forest.

It was early evening when Joshua and the handful of other new draftees who'd traveled with him walked through the gates and reported for duty. They were ordered to put on their armbands and were then led past rows of wooden barracks to join their unit, which was housed in low bunkers dug into the ground and covered by roofs topped with sod, making them hard to spot from the air.

Joshua's small group was met outside the bunker by a sergeant, a gorilla of a man in his late twenties, who clearly had no need to befriend the Jews under his command. He growled a list of his expectations for the men, threatening harsh consequences for any insubordination. "Do what you're supposed to, and you just might live out the war. Disobey me, and you probably won't," he advised. He ordered them to go inside, claim places to sleep, and stand by them, at attention, until he came to check their papers and search their bags.

There were no individual bunks in the bunker, just two long rows of wooden shelves, covered with about an inch of lice-infested straw. The kerosene lamps were lit, and weary-looking men were lounging and sitting on the shelves, some reading, others playing cards, some resting their eyes. They greeted the fresh arrivals with expressions of curiosity mixed with pity. Joshua was struck at once by how lean the veteran laborers were. He found a space that was unoccupied, put his suitcase there, and waited.

He watched the sergeant go down the line, inspecting the papers of each new draftee, then searching their bags and confiscating anything that appealed to him, mostly food and money. As their possessions were stolen, the young men's faces registered protest, but they said nothing. At last, the sergeant stood before Joshua.

"Identification," he demanded.

Joshua handed over his ID booklet, and the sergeant opened it. His eyes widened in confusion. He looked at Joshua, then back at the ID book, then back at Joshua.

"What is this?" the sergeant asked, hesitatingly.

"That's my friend," Joshua answered. Inside his ID book, he'd tucked the inscribed photograph of the Hungarian general with whom he'd shared a hospital room over ten years earlier. The sergeant was dumbfounded. To soldiers, generals were viewed as gods. The sergeant's disposition changed instantly, his harshness replaced by amicability. He handed the papers back to Joshua, saying, "I'm sure there's no need for me to search your things. If you have any problems or questions, let me know." From that moment on, Joshua was treated with just enough deference to remind him that he was human.

⸺❖⸺

Every morning, the men were given a cup of weak coffee and half a loaf of bread for the day. Every evening, they were served a gruel of green and yellow peas, and if they were lucky, got one of the few tidbits of meat used to flavor the soup; my grandfather ate so many peas while in the labor corps that, after the war, he couldn't stomach them ever again. It was hardly enough to fuel the men during their long days of slaving on the airfield.

Joshua spent the first couple of months of his service at a nearby quarry, blasting rocks out of the earth with dynamite, hacking them to pieces with picks, then shoveling the rubble into wagons. These were pulled, sometimes by horses, sometimes by men, down a narrow muddy path to the construction site, where crews laid them down into what would become a runway. He was skinny to begin with, and not very strong. He struggled with the weight of the pick, able to deliver only a few blows before pausing for breath. His hands, though rough from working wood, blistered and bled for weeks before they callused. His arms remained thin, but became sinewy. His clothing became embedded with rock dust and sweat. His close-cropped hair was a haven for lice. The men were worked to their breaking points—and more than a few collapsed from injury or exhaustion— but keeping in mind the tales he'd heard of Jewish laborers on the Russian front, Joshua knew things could be a lot worse.

The commander of the camp had once led a labor battalion in Ukraine and had a notorious reputation. He had sent scores of Jews across minefields, and, being a drunkard, hadn't interfered when his sergeants amused themselves by torturing their crews. He was regarded as fickle, unpredictable, and violent. With so many laborers under his authority, those in Joshua's unit just hoped they'd go more or less unnoticed. Once, however, not long after Joshua began his service, the commander paid a visit to the bunker and ordered all of the laborers to line up outside.

"Jews!" he shouted. "You're all a bunch of stinking scum and don't you forget it!" A palpable tension coursed through the unit as the men imagined what might come next. The commander, however, surprised them by adding, "But if any guard raises a hand against you, you can come directly to me to report it. I give you permission to break the chain of command. I tolerate no insubordination!" Now that he was stationed in Hungary and was subject to official oversight, the commander strictly obeyed the army's directives regarding the welfare of its laborers.

Winter arrived in early November. Lifting rough, heavy stones with chapped and icy hands, even Joshua's calluses cracked and oozed; swinging his pick with extra vigor in order to stay warm, he worked up a sweat that froze the moment he took a rest; pulling a wagon alongside two horses, he slipped in the snow and was nearly crushed by a wheel. So when his sergeant announced that a crew was needed to repair the camp's many barracks, Joshua volunteered immediately. His journeyman's carpentry certificate proved he was as skilled as he was willing, and earned him the status of crew chief.

Instantly, life got easier. The repair crews were barely supervised, so they agreed among themselves to look very busy without actually getting much done. As they fixed some things, they broke others, which they would then have to repair. Since the barracks had woodstoves, they would burn shelving and even bunks, keeping themselves warm, then requisition more wood to rebuild what they'd dismantled. The way my grandfather describes the situation, it sounds like he spent the winter in an episode of *Hogan's Heroes*.

Soon after he began working on the barracks, the sergeant came to Joshua's crew asking if anyone knew how to repair a typewriter, since the one in the camp's administrative office had broken. Joshua said that he did, that his father had run a printing business. He was taken to the office, where he examined the typewriter. He could fix it, he said, but he'd need a few parts, and was given a pass to go into Veszprem to get them. As with the barracks, when Joshua fixed the typewriter, he weakened another part, so it would break before long, giving him a reason to go back into town. Before each trip, he'd collect money from his bunkmates and return with chocolate bars and wedges of cheese hidden in his clothing; he took no commission, he says, preferring to make friends rather than profit.

The Hungarians who ran the office came to realize that Joshua was educated and bright, and soon asked him to help out with paperwork. As they came to trust him, they began leaving him there alone, with unguarded access to files and supplies, including blank passes. In January 1944, Joshua stole a pass, wrote himself a week's leave, and forged a signature. He slipped out of camp and headed for Veszprem, from where he intended to take a train home to see his family.

Before he got to the station, however, he encountered an army patrol. The commanding officer asked to see his pass. Joshua handed it to him, trying to conceal his anxiety. It wasn't that unusual for Jewish laborers to be given leave; they were now treated more or less like legitimate members of the army, able to receive letters and packages, paid a token salary of about a dollar a week, and every so often, allowed to go home. But as the officer examined the pass, he squinted his eyes in skepticism.

"What the hell is this?" he exclaimed. "This pass was written for January 1943!" Apparently, Joshua had written the wrong year on the pass out of habit.

"I don't know," he replied nervously. "That's what they gave me."

"Let me see your papers," the officer demanded.

Joshua gave him his ID book and, once again, the photo of the general had a magical effect. The officer stared at it in surprise, then flipped it closed and handed it back. "Whoever wrote this pass is an idiot," he pronounced. "Have a good week."

For the rest of my grandfather's life, stealing this pass remained among the things he'd done for which he was most grateful. The days he spent with his family were filled with affection and intellectual conversation, talk of his father's latest efforts to get food and clothing to Jewish labor units on the front lines, bowls of his mother's borscht, and the amusing outbursts of his sister. He went back to his unit heartened and refreshed, with no idea that he would never see any of them again. His only pressing concern about the future was the punishment he might face for going AWOL.

TWENTY-EIGHT

For my grandmother, 1943 is but a blur. One day merged into the next, with little to distinguish them from each other. Neither she nor her friend Renee has any specific memories from that year. When asked about it, both give nearly identical replies. "What were we doing? Trying to survive!" Life remained a struggle, yet, having endured the extreme agonies of the previous years, the daily quest to outwit starvation had become an activity as mundane as it was heroic. They'd succumbed to the monotony of misery, which helped desensitize them to some of its worst manifestations. Hunger and cold were accepted as the norm. The daily news of yet another dead Jew was met with little emotion, unless they'd been particularly close to that person. Life was taken a day at a time. Even talking between themselves, Renee and Isadora were careful not to speak too often of their hopes and dreams for the future—partly for fear of jinxing them, and partly because imagining better times only brought into clearer focus just how bad the present was.

With the war having turned decisively against the Germans by the summer of 1943, Antonescu began to consider the wisdom of bringing the deportees back to

Romania, yet couldn't swallow the idea of a general repatriation. Over the course of many months, lists defining which categories of Jews might be granted reentry were drawn up, scratched out, and rewritten. Government officials began negotiating with Zionist groups and concerned foreign governments, seeking to ransom the lives of orphaned children for thousands of dollars a head. They also worked out deals with the Zionists to transport the orphans on to Palestine, preferring they didn't stay in Romania.

At last, at the end of February 1944, Antonescu sent out teams to rescue those children under fifteen who had lost both parents. Both Isadora, now nineteen, and Yisrael, now seventeen, were too old to qualify.

When three representatives from Jewish relief agencies arrived in Obodovka, word spread among the Jews nearly as quickly as the typhus epidemic. Everyone, it seemed, came out to watch as the men, dressed in heavy coats and hats, wearing boots, walked down the snow-covered streets, stopping at each house to look for orphans who met the criteria set by the government. They couldn't mask their shock, their faces expressing both horror at finding a community forced to live in such ragged destitution, and astonishment that anyone had been able to endure it for so long. The Jews of Obodovka looked upon the rescuers with awe, as though they were angels of mercy rather than human beings like themselves. Perhaps, many hoped, if the orphans were allowed back into Romania, others would soon be able to follow. But no one knew for sure.

Parents pleaded with the men to take their children, even though they weren't orphans. Though it was painful for them to refuse, the rescuers feared that any improprieties in their selections might be discovered, jeopardizing the entire operation. When they came near enough for Isadora to see their faces, she recognized one of them at once. She ran up to him, grabbed his dark woolen sleeve, and breathlessly sputtered, "Mr. Tomarkin, Mr. Tomarkin!" He looked down at her, perplexed, unable to register who she might be.

"It's me, Isa Rosen," she said, "Mitzi Iacobescu's niece." Tomarkin, a lawyer, had been a friend of the family when they'd lived in Balti, and had been lucky enough to be away in Bucharest when Bessarabia had been occupied.

Tomarkin examined her face, which was a few years older and much, much thinner than it had been, and said, "My God." He cradled her head against his chest and held her, as much for his own comfort as for hers. When he returned with her to the barn she was living in, she recounted the main events of the last few years—how her mother, one aunt, and one uncle had died in the ghetto; how Mitzi had been arrested and her other uncles had disappeared, and that all were probably dead.

Tomarkin told Isadora that he was getting her and Yisrael out of there. "If anyone asks how old you are, tell them 'fifteen,' " he said. She was so gaunt, no one at a glance would be able to tell whether she was twenty or twelve.

Isadora ran to Renee's house, where she found Renee sitting on the floor, kneading a lump of dough on a smooth old board, a bundle of skinny sticks piled by the dormant fireplace behind her. "I'm leaving!" Isadora exclaimed.

"What? How?" Renee said, dropping the dough and leaping to her feet.

Isadora explained, and she and Renee hugged each other tightly, laughing and crying in a confused burst of emotions. They would each be losing a friend as beloved as a sister, yet were overjoyed that one of them would at last be free. Isadora said teary, excited good-byes to Martin and Renee's mother, hugged Renee once more, and then left to find Onu. He shed no tears, just smiled sweetly, kissed her on the cheek, and sent her off with his latest poem. The Parnas family, she imagines, was sad to see her go, but happy she was going. My grandmother has absolutely no memory of these people who took her in; everything she knows about them she was told by her brother, who was astonished that she'd completely forgotten them.

The following day, she and Yisrael climbed in the back of a horse-drawn cart filled with other parentless children from the village, and headed west, toward Moghilev, crossing the Dniester in early March. In Atachi, they were dropped at the railroad tracks, deloused, and herded into cattle cars for the train ride to Iasi. Isadora lost all contact with her friends from Obodovka, and had no way of finding them again.

Days after Isadora left Transnistria, the region was flooded with German troops retreating from the Soviet onslaught. Thousands of Jews were murdered by the Nazis, under the pretense that they were a security threat. Antonescu, afraid that he'd be held accountable by the Allies for the latest round of massacres, issued orders to evacuate the remaining deportees, but it was too late. Within two weeks, Transnistria was completely in Russian hands. Only then did Renee, her mother, Martin, and Onu manage to escape, sneaking back over the Dniester before the border was sealed by the Soviets.

Onu eventually settled in Bucharest, becoming an editor at a large newspaper, as well as a protégé of the poet, Paul Celan. Renee married Martin, and the couple eventually immigrated to the United States. When they were living in Westchester County, New York, decades after the war ended, Renee and Martin were at the home of a friend who was hosting a small dinner party. They were drinking wine and chatting, when another couple was welcomed through the front door.

Upon seeing them, the woman who'd just arrived walked straight up to Martin and, before being introduced, said, "I know you."

"How do you know me?" Martin asked.

"From Obodovka," the woman answered.

"Obodovka?!" Martin and Renee both exclaimed, and Renee asked, "Who are you?"

"I was Isadora Rosen," my grandmother said.

So much time had passed that she and Renee had barely recognized each other. They embraced with the vigor of shipwrecked sailors clinging to a drifting plank and broke down in tears. They were speechless, then words tumbled forth in a disorderly tumult, with more to say than they could figure out how to express. That night they again became the closest of friends and remain so to this day.

TWENTY-NINE

The bus rattled and groaned its way across the Ukrainian countryside, its vinyl-covered benches saggy and torn, its once-white walls dented, scuffed, and smudged with what looked like soot. I sat in the back, surrounded by a group of Gypsies in their teens and twenties; their high spirits, eclectic attire, and musky aroma reminded me of a clan of devoted Deadheads weeks into following their favorite band around on its summer tour. I'd been warned by many people, both at home and in Romania, to beware of the Gypsies; that they were masters at using their natural charms to disarm even the most wary of marks; and that, before I knew it, they'd make my money vanish from my pockets as though they had the powers of crooked David Copperfields. I didn't know how much truth existed behind these allegations, but it seemed wise not to buy into the worst rumors about people before actually meeting them.

These Gypsies *were* charming. Attracted by the uncommon sight of a tourist on this bus route, they were eager to engage, and before long, despite the language difficulties, we were laughing together. The young men were gregarious and playful, most wearing faded jeans and black leather vests over multicolored wool sweaters. The women, hair covered in embroidered scarves, were lively, with smiles that were alluring without trying to be, and hands that remained graceful despite their roughness. When they learned I was unmarried, one of the men suggested, without a shred of seriousness, that I take the oldest of the women—who must've been about twenty-five—as a wife. She smiled and blushed, and I played along as though it was an appealing possibility. We discussed dowries, and I learned that I'd begin my married life as the proud new owner of a milk cow and a bed in her family's home. When the bus pulled over to the side of the road, seemingly in the middle of nowhere, the Gypsies gathered their burlap bundles, we wished each other well, and they got off. They'd performed no acts of underhanded magic.

Changing buses in Iampol, a town along the Dniester south of Moghilev and another infamous crossing point for deported Romanian Jews during the war, I learned that few buses passed through Obodovka, which was not on the main route to anywhere. Once I got there, I'd have no way of leaving until the following day, and the town was so small that it had no hotels. I bought my ticket anyway, certain I'd be able to find somewhere to spend the night.

The bus trundled over the rolling terrain that my grandmother had marched across sixty-four years earlier. Covered with farm plots and grassy ranges, the land was open to the full onslaught of the elements, with no natural shelter from sun or wind, rain, snow, or cold. I was struck by how exposed my grandmother and her companions must have felt, especially under the brutal conditions they endured. This day was sunny and cloudless, though the sky was stained by smoke from the smoldering fields.

As I stared out the window, I contemplated the significance of this pilgrimage I was undertaking. Going to Obodovka was, for me, like visiting Auschwitz. I felt that I should do something to pay my respects to my family members who had perished there, as well as to commemorate my grandmother's own near-death ordeal. But I couldn't think of a thing. I'm not a religious person. I'd never met those who died. Any ritual I imagined performing, either semi-traditional or completely improvised, would have felt phony. And the scale of the suffering that had taken place there would have dwarfed anything I attempted to do into meaninglessness. By the time the bus stopped in Obodovka, I'd given up on the idea.

The bus stop was a small stone and cinder-block building with two benches outside and one room inside that housed the ticket office. At the barred window, I asked if there was a hotel in town, and was told there wasn't. I then asked if I could I leave my backpack in the ticket office for a while, while I walked around. No, I was told; the bus stop was closing in a few minutes. Questions answered, I shouldered my bag and set out to explore, hoping to absorb something of the essence of the place. No one in my family had been there since my grandmother was rescued from it, and I doubted anyone would be again.

Except for the main paved road, the few streets are made of pebbly dirt, lined by simple white houses with tin roofs steeply pitched to shed the winter snows. Each has a yard and a vegetable garden, bound by wooden fences threaded with morning-glory vines. Territorial mutts patrol the yards, snarling fiercely at the random passerby, who stays well clear of the fence. A forest covers the hillside behind the town, while before it lies a collage of meadows and farmland, spreading across a shallow valley. Few people were out. There was a woman with her preteen daughter, each wearing plain long dresses and rubber boots, carrying sticks the length of fishing poles. They scampered behind nine willful cows that dragged long, heavy chains fastened around their necks and resisted being herded onto the lawn in front of the local school. There were three drunk guys riding in a horse-drawn wagon that stopped to offer me a ride. There was the rare car that drove by on the main road.

As the afternoon grew late, I followed a footpath to a spot in the valley away from all the houses, where the creek had been dammed to form a small lake. Long-horned cows grazed nearby. Squadrons of swallows swooped low over the reservoir in an erratic black cloud that condensed and expanded, then shot off toward the horizon. It was quiet, perfectly peaceful. As the sun went down, it glowed like a hot round coal, searing the sky orange, which was mirrored in the gently rippling surface of the water. There was nothing inherently evil about Obodovka, I saw; it was just an innocent place where some evil business went down.

When it got dark, I went to the town's one restaurant, across the street from the bus stop. Tables covered with peach-colored cloths were arranged around a linoleum dance floor. Except for one family eating across the room, the place was empty. A waitress brought me a menu from the bar, and I ordered modestly, careful as always of my budget. While I waited for my food, the restaurant began to fill up. The stereo was turned on. Pop music pumped from the speakers, and a few of the local girls began to dance with each other, wearing heels and short, tight dresses, looking like they'd been transported from a club in Moscow.

When my food arrived, it hit me after the first few bites. The thing I was looking for, to pay tribute to my family members . . . was eating. After so many Jews had died there of starvation, after my grandmother had lived for weeks on a diet of boiled straw, that I could go to Obodovka and stuff myself just by asking for food was a victory, the most vivid symbol of my family's survival that I could imagine. It was the one thing I could do that felt appropriate, authentic, and meaningful. I called the waitress back and ordered a chicken.

The knowledge of what had brought me to this unremarkable Ukrainian village slammed into me, full force, knocking me into a hyperemotional state. Grieving sharply over the past, profoundly grateful for the present, I savored every mouthful with tears brimming in my eyes, flooded with feelings of loss and triumph—and hoping no one at the restaurant was paying much attention to the stranger getting misty-eyed over a roasted chicken. I was overcome with the sense that it had been very right for me to have gone to Obodovka, like some long unfinished business had finally been wrapped up. Even if I had to spend the night outside, I thought, it'd be worth it.

I decided to linger at the restaurant for a while, figuring it would be the most likely place for me to meet someone who might offer a place to stay. I moved to one of the tables out on the patio, drinking tea and petting a stray three-legged dog. The night grew colder; I could see my breath, and pressed my hands against the teapot for warmth. After an hour or so passed with no luck, and I was beginning to lose hope, I met a man who spoke a little English. When he learned that I was from America and, at that point, planned to pass the night at the bus stop, he was aghast. If I had to sleep outside for lack of a room, it would reflect terribly on the hospitality of Obodovkans, he thought. He led me to a wooden kiosk the size of an Airstream—which sold snacks, cigarettes, and booze—and asked the shop owner if she had a room I could rent. The woman, who appeared to be in her fifties, looked me over and said yes, for ten bucks. She hollered something out the kiosk window, and soon a young woman in a red leather jacket appeared; she was given some instructions, and led me to the house, about two minutes away. She kept a few paces ahead of me, with no apparent interest in talking.

There were two people at the house when we got there—a man in his mid-twenties, and a boy who looked to be about seven. Though by this time it was about 10:00 P.M., the man was busy tiling the walls in the kitchen, which was a mess of construction materials and debris. He greeted me warmly, though didn't want me to shake his mastic-covered hands, smiling a welcome instead through the cement dust coating his face. He had a friendly, laid-back way about him, and I liked him at once. The boy, with golden hair, wearing a filthy green sweater with a heart in the center, was a pure joy, laughing with delight every time I looked at him. I was shown my room: the gray floor was gritty with dirt, the turquoise-colored walls were coated with grime, the brown blanket on the bed, which bore a huge image of a tiger's face, clearly hadn't been washed in a long time. But I'd slept in worse places before, recognized it was sheer luxury compared to my grandmother's roofless shed, and the kindness of my hosts more than compensated for the grunge.

While I was playing with the boy, feeling relaxed and content, a man and a woman arrived at the house, both drunk to the point of slurring and stumbling slightly. He looked to be about thirty; she, with a heavily weathered face and callused, cigarette-stained fingers, looked old enough to have been his mother. The guy, however, cleared up any confusion I might've had about the nature of their relationship by grabbing the woman and mock-humping her from behind. The woman yelled at my seven-year-old playmate to get out of the room, as though he was nothing but a nuisance simply because he was child. I sat on the edge of the bed as the two strangers hovered over me so closely that I could smell the alcohol on their breath, underneath the plumes of smoke they exhaled, while they questioned me persistently in a language I couldn't understand.

I had an instant aversion to them. My instincts told me that these people were bad news. But, I told myself, there was nothing much to worry myself about; they'd most likely be leaving in a few minutes after they got bored with me. I just had to be patient and wait them out, and then the happy little household would return to itself. I was wrong. The drunks were staying for the night, and the tile man and the boy were leaving. I didn't like it. Something just didn't feel right. I tried to quiet my concerns with my mind. Maybe these people were a little bit creepy, but they hadn't actually done anything menacing. Nothing bad had happened, and I told myself that nothing would. Unable to shake my intuitions—yet not wanting to overreact—I moved my backpack to the head of the bed to deter possible pilfering, then tried to go to sleep.

Just as I was finally drifting off, I was awakened by shouting in the other bedroom. He was yelling at her, she was screaming back at him. I tried to ignore it and fall back asleep, thinking they'd quiet down in a minute. Then I heard the unmistakable thuds of fists pounding flesh, and her wailing in pain. In a matter of seconds, I was up. I quickly packed my things, shouldered my bag, and headed for the door. The only way out, however, was through their bedroom. I hoped that walking in on them would interrupt the assault, but I had no backup plan in case it didn't. I'd never been in a fistfight in my adult life, and wanted to keep it that way.

I opened the door to their room and stepped in. She was lying on the bed, crying, with blood on her face; he stood over her, his body taut. The instant he saw me, his face fell and he backed away from her. He held up his hands in a gesture of innocence, and urged me to go back to my room. Sensing that, for the moment at least, the beating had been suspended, I had no qualms about beelining it for the door. He followed me outside, trailing a step behind, shouting at me to return to the house. I kept cool, calmly saying in English that everything was okay, as if I was trying to soothe a growling Rottweiler, more with my tone than my words. As he shadowed me down the street, his anger turned to pleading, as though something personal was at stake for him if I left. I kept walking, with even, rapid strides, back to the small shop run by the woman who'd rented me the room in the first place. Fortunately, she was still there.

I went inside, explained the situation, and got my money back. She then turned to the abusive drunk and gave him such an epic tongue-lashing that his entire body went limp with shame. Maybe *she* was his mother. She was still berating him as I left, and I fantasized that word about the incident would spread through the village, earning him the scorn of his neighbors, embarrassing him into changing his ways. (Like I said, it was a fantasy.)

With no other options, I headed for the bus stop. The sky was clear and moonless. The stars dazzled, points of pure light against a field of absolute black. Though a little shaken by my brush with domestic brutality, I wasn't distraught at being homeless for the night. Besides, something about being out in the freezing cold in this place helped me get a better feel for my grandmother's experiences than did knowing what it was like to be cold in some other place. And it *was* cold. Once my adrenaline wore off and I began to feel it, I dug more clothing out of my pack. I knew I had little to complain about, since these temperatures would have been balmy compared with those my grandmother endured. Even forgetting for a minute the typhus epidemic that consumed Obodovka, I found it hard to imagine anyone simply surviving the winter.

Around two in the morning, the young woman with the red leather jacket who had led me to the wife-beater's house passed by

with a friend. She saw me, and they came over to find out what was
going on. I recounted the evening's drama for them and, in the process, found we connected easily. We talked for a while, frequently
breaking into laughter. They were both nineteen, and clearly—or
so my instincts said—good people. She laughed with depth and
had a smile so pure it sparked a flare of happiness in me whenever
she showed it. The guy she was with was slightly intoxicated, just
enough to enhance his natural exuberance. After nearly an hour had
passed, the tipsy young man offered to take me to his house, in the
next village. I could ride on the back of his motorcycle, which had
no headlight, while wearing my pack. I thanked him, and said it
sounded like a bad idea. The girl agreed, and invited me to her place
instead, which was less than a minute's walk away.

She lived in a small house behind the bus station. When we
stepped inside, she said we'd have to be quiet, so we wouldn't wake
her one-year-old. The child's father, she explained, had split before
the baby was born, and she had never heard from him again. The
house had two rooms and a kitchen. In the first room, where the
child slept, a laundry line was strung, from which hung socks, a
couple of blouses, and baby clothes. In the dim light, I could see that
aside from the bed, the only other furniture was a chest of drawers
and a small round table with no chairs. Her mother slept on a mattress in the kitchen. The cement floors were uncarpeted. A handful
of blurry photographs of people were taped to the walls in random
places, along with two pictures torn from magazines, one of snow-
capped mountains, the other of kittens.

She offered me her bed, which occupied every inch of space in
the other room, saying she'd sleep with the child. I accepted with
thanks, said good-night, and lay down. Springs poked through the
mattress, which reeked of cat piss, but I didn't care. That this young
woman, who had practically nothing but a child, would open her

home to a stranger in the middle of the night gave me comfort beyond the material, made me warmer than being inside, sheltered me in the most profound of ways. Such generosity was unimaginable when my grandmother was there. But I had found goodness in Obodovka, and I was glad. ❧

THIRTY

When Joshua returned to his unit from his self-granted leave, his sergeant pulled him aside. "I know you were gone," he said. "Without permission." Joshua remained silent. "If you try it again, even a photo of Horthy himself won't save you. Get it?"

"Yes, sir," Joshua answered, relieved that he wasn't going to be punished. He would never try his luck again. Soon, there was nowhere to go, and Jewish men would be clamoring to get *in* to the army's labor camps.

Impatient with Hungary's resistance to participating in the Final Solution, and doubting its loyalty to the Axis, Germany occupied its ally on March 19, 1944. Within days, Adolf Eichmann—the SS leader in charge of Jewish deportations and the head of the Gestapo's Department of Jewish Affairs—set up shop in Budapest's Majestic Hotel. He'd come to deal with the Jewish Question in Hungary himself. Within weeks, plans for rounding up the country's Jews and shipping them to concentration camps had been drawn.

The deportations would take place in stages, beginning with Subcarpathia and Northern Transylvania. The Jews living there would be told that they were being moved away from the front lines because they were thought to be Bolshevik sympathizers and a security threat. Most Jews, Eichmann correctly predicted, had grown so accustomed to these kinds of accusations that they'd believe it really was the motive for relocating them, and wouldn't perceive anything ominous behind it. Even the most sympathetic Gentile wouldn't raise a voice against moving Jews out of a military zone. Meanwhile, Eichmann would convince the Jews in the rest of the country that the actions would be limited to the territories taken from Czechoslovakia and Romania, and that they, as true Hungarians, wouldn't be touched. After Subcarpathia and Transylvania had been cleansed, deportations would begin in rural Hungary, sweep through the country, and end with Budapest—by which time the Jewish elite living in the capital would have nowhere to escape to.

German and Hungarian squads descended upon the Subcarpathian countryside at the break of dawn on April 16, 1944. It was the first day of Passover. In small villages across the province, Jews were given just minutes to pack a suitcase, told to bring only a single change of clothes, any blankets or pillows they might want, and no more than two weeks' worth of food. Valuables and livestock were to be left behind. They were then marched and driven by wagon to transit camps just outside the nearest city that had a rail line. Within two days, some 15,000 Jews who lived near Uzhgorod had been packed into a brick factory about a mile outside the city. For a few days, Uzhgorod's Jews supplied their rural brethren with food, but then they, too, were herded into the brickyard. Bela, Berta, and Aviva were among them.

The factory grounds were spacious enough to comfortably contain about 2,000 people. Aside from an area the size of half a basketball court, which was covered by an awning, the yard was open to the sky. Families tried to erect makeshift shelters, or at least get a little privacy, by dry-stacking whatever bricks they could scavenge and improvising tents from blankets and tablecloths. Most, however, claimed a patch of bare ground with nothing over their heads. For a short time, Uzhgorod's police chief helped smuggle food into the camp, until he was kicked off the force by Hungarian authorities. Afterward, people began to slowly starve. A Jewish council was responsible for feeding everyone in the camp and each day managed to provide a few bites of bread and two cups of watery potato soup to all. There was no running water and no toilet. Pit latrines were dug out in plain view—one of many humiliations to be endured.

The gendarmes picked a corner of the brickyard in which they set up a "mint"—a *plein air* torture chamber where prisoners were persuaded to reveal where they had stashed their jewelry and their gold. Guards amused themselves with their prisoners, once commanding a group of Orthodox men to don their prayer shawls and pray. Moments after beginning their devotions, they were beaten bloody with sticks and fists. While writhing on the ground, crying in pain, their beards and *peyes* were shorn off. One of these men, so ashamed of his beardless face, covered it with a scarf for the rest of his stay in the factory.

Though the Jews generally helped each other out, there was also plenty of arguing, often about what was fated for them. Some insisted on believing the story told by the Hungarians—that they were being sent to work on farms a few hours to the south, near Debrecen. Others knew that something worse awaited them. During the first week of May, word leaked in to the factory's Jewish Council about a report written in Slovakia by one Rudolf Vrba, who had escaped from Auschwitz. The report detailed everything from the gas chambers to the crematoria, to the process used by the Nazis to select who would live and who would die. Among the council members, opinion was split about whether or not to believe the report; it seemed simply impossible. The council agreed to keep the story silent, fearing that revealing it would produce a general panic, the consequences of which could be worse than whatever unknown future awaited them.

By mid-May, conditions in the brick factory had become subhuman; the filth, the stench, the hunger, and the illness had all become overwhelming. And most would never have it so good again. On May 15, the first groups were led from the brick factory to the train station, where they were packed into cattle cars and sent off to Auschwitz. Bela, Berta, and Aviva were taken the following day.

On April 20, 1944, a day or two before they were rounded up and taken to the brickyard, Joshua's family wrote him a letter. Clearly, they had no illusions about what was taking place. The letter reads:

> *My Dearest Son,*
>
> *With the minimum necessities we are all packed, as are all the Jews of the town, to be shipped, in accordance with the orders of the Hungarian government, to an unknown destination for unknown purposes.*
>
> *The Jews from the countryside were brought into the local brick factory, some 10,000 souls, your grandmother and Aunt Malvin among them. For a number of days, the Jews of the town fed them, but now that we are also ready to be shipped out, there will be nobody to care for them. Probably our fate will be the same.*
>
> Berta continues: *We are already a week on death row. Your cousin Bill was home on leave from the labor battalion. He arrived the day before yesterday. He walked from Chop, and on the way*

he ran into the wagon that was bringing his family to the brick factory—he even managed to visit with them, with a special pass, and today he left. If he will have a chance, he will find you later.

Unfortunately we have no hope. We are only permitted two dresses and underwear, one on our body and one packed. It seems we will have no need of the clothes for long.

I am strong, and have closed the book on my life. You are now an adult and can take care of yourself. I only feel sorry for Aviva. I only wish she shouldn't have to suffer. I don't believe in God anymore, since if this can happen, I cannot believe, therefore I do not say "God be with you." It is possible that we might write again.

Bela continues: I mailed you a hundred pengo, and gave Bill another hundred to give you one day. I sent some of your clothes with Bill, too. We shipped you two good watches and a gold ring. I hope they arrive.

There are rumors that they will transfer us to the Danube region, or perhaps to Debrecen. We will write to you from wherever we are, if we're alive.

From my book, eleven sheets are printed and the twelfth one is set. If once this is all over we are not alive anymore, try to publish the book, if there will be anyone left to publish for. This might give you an income for some time. Of course, there will need to be a postscript describing these happenings.

Thereafter, try to get to our ancient homeland, and live there an honorable life, sanctifying our memory. Never turn away from our national ideals; be a thoughtful and sincere fighter for our rights. Do not despair. Do not be sad. Do not mourn. Perhaps we will survive. But, should we be annihilated, remember—nobody can live forever. We would have to die anyhow; it just happened somewhat sooner this way. You try to get along the best you can.

Your Loving Father.

A postscript from Aviva, written at the bottom of the page, reads:

> *Dear Joshua,*
>
> *Unfortunately, we will not have it anymore as good as we once did. I think that you are the lucky one. This might be the last time I'm writing to you. My braids are cut.*
>
> *A thousand kisses, with love, your pity-deserving sister.*

Berta and Aviva were gassed upon arrival at Auschwitz. Bela was deemed fit for work and transferred to the concentration camp at Mauthausen.

THIRTY-ONE

At about the same time that Bela, Berta, and Aviva were moved to the Uzhgorod brickyard, Isadora and Yisrael were transferred from a temporary camp in Iasi—where they were fed, clothed, and bathed—to an orphanage in Bucharest, with a group of other children who had lost their parents in Transnistria. Housed in a two-story building, the orphans slept ten to a room, with separate wings for boys and girls. Kosher food was served in the dining hall, which was staffed by some of the older orphans. Other children did laundry, cleaned rooms, or babysat the littlest ones. The place had an institutional feel, more like a hospital than a home, but Isadora and Yisrael weren't complaining.

Within days of arriving, Isadora contacted her extended family members who lived in Bucharest. These included a couple of uncles, a few aunts, and her paternal grandmother; they had never left the city and endured only minor inconveniences during the war. Isa had never been close to them, as they had always scorned her family as nothing more than a bunch of country bumpkins. Now, as she returned parentless from Transnistria, they welcomed her with ambivalence. They were as thrilled to see her as if she'd been away for a weekend. No one offered to take her or her brother in; they didn't have enough room, they said. Isadora returned to the orphanage, brokenhearted.

Before long, she revealed her true age to the caretakers of the orphanage. Understanding that she had nothing, they agreed to let her stay, but said she'd have to earn her keep. They found her a job as a nurse's aide in the maternity ward of a Jewish hospital, and she handed her small salary over to the orphanage. She loved her job; she had a keen appreciation for the value of human life, and helping to deliver newborns felt like an affirmation that there was still goodness and innocence in this world. Yisrael, meanwhile, put the skills he'd acquired in Obodovka to good use and spent his days on the streets as an agent in Bucharest's black market.

Occasionally they would have dinner at their uncle Herman's spacious apartment. The owner of a clothing store that somehow managed to stay open for business, he would invite them to come by the shop, offering them 30 percent off of anything they wanted. Dressed in hand-me-downs donated by strangers, Isadora and Yisrael knew that even with the discount, they still wouldn't be able to afford anything their uncle sold. Inevitably during dinner, the subject of Isadora and Yisrael's future would arise. They should really go to Palestine, their family urged, along with many of the other orphans. It was a place of full of possibility, and they had nothing worth staying for in Bucharest. It might have been true, but Isadora didn't want to go; she just wanted her family to take them in.

"As soon as they brought up Palestine, I couldn't eat," my grandmother remembered. "The food just stuck in my throat."

In November 1944, a representative from the Jewish Agency came to the orphanage, offering the children a chance to immigrate to Palestine. A boat, he said, would be sailing from Constanta within a few weeks. Isadora, by this time convinced that her family would never adopt her and her brother, considered it. She didn't envision life in Bucharest getting much better anytime soon, and she worried about Yisrael's ever-deepening involvement in the city's underworld. If she was to obey her mother's dying request, she had to steer her brother away from his budding criminal career. Though she had no concrete hopes for what they would find there and had never given much thought to Zionism, Isa wasn't immune to the mystique of Palestine; after all, it was the Promised Land, and thus by definition *had* to be better than Bucharest.

On the first day of December, she and Yisrael each packed a small bag; they knew how to travel light, and didn't own much anyway. With hundreds of other Jewish orphans from around the city, they boarded a train for the coast.

THIRTY-TWO

When Joshua received his parents' last letter, he didn't know what to think. He was angered by their deportation, devastated by the loss of their home, and deeply concerned by his parents' predictions of their imminent deaths. But he had never heard of Auschwitz or any of the other death camps, and wouldn't for another five months or so. That tens of thousands of people who lived around Uzhgorod could simply be annihilated was too boggling to believe, so he clung to the hope that they'd be reunited once the war was over. He, for the moment, was safe, since Jewish labor servicemen were off limits to Eichmann's *Sonderkommando* units and the Hungarian gendarmes who worked with them.

Over the summer of 1944, Joshua's entire company was transferred to a sawmill at Alesd, in Northern Transylvania, between the Romanian cities of Oradea and Cluj-Napoca. The forested Plopisului Mountains rose behind the northern side of the town; to the south, the flat, fertile Crisul Repede valley spread to a horizon line darkly rippled by the Apuseni Mountains. The mill, owned by the Swiss company LaRoche, had been converted to produce prefabricated barracks for the German army. Crews of Jews, who would operate the factory alongside teams of Romanian slave laborers, arrived a few days before the plant was to begin operating. Joshua stood in a slow-moving line of hundreds waiting to enter the camp, as the commander—who was a Romanian hussar in World War I, and wore the red pants and tall boots unique to that elite cavalry corps—greeted the men in the company individually, making them pause as they came through the gate so he could kick each of them once, hard, in the seat of the pants.

In the predawn hours of the morning that the factory was scheduled to start production, guards burst into Joshua's barracks, turning on the lights and shouting, shaking the bunks. "Get up and get outside!" they ordered, slapping the heaviest sleepers with wooden batons. Rumpled, weary, and afraid, the Jews were lined up in a dusty, barren yard ringed by machine guns mounted on tripods. Forced to stand at attention, they watched quietly as the sky glowed in anticipation of sunrise. One at a time, alphabetically by last name and with long intervals in between, they were taken away without being told why, and none who were removed returned to the yard. It turned out that the factory's generators had been sabotaged. Had the mischief gone undiscovered before the main switch was thrown, the whole plant might have blown up. The laborers were being interrogated individually in a quest to uncover the culprits.

Since Joshua's last name began with "Sz," he waited for hours for his name to be called. As the morning wore on, he remained standing at attention in the unshaded yard while the sun grew hot. By the time they'd gotten to the Rs, he'd begun to nod off. At last, his tired head slipped. In an instant, a guard was beside him, ordering him back to attention, and demanding to know why Joshua had a smile on his face. Joshua said he wasn't sure, he must've been dreaming a little.

"I'll give you something to dream about," the guard said, and picked two pebbles off the ground. "Hold these," he said. "Now stick out your arms, and squat." He unholstered his pistol and pointed it at Joshua's head. "Don't drop them," the guard said.

Joshua maintained his stance for what felt like an eternity. As he felt his muscles quiver, he'd muster his strength and hold them firm again. At last, he had nothing left, and his arms fell to his sides. The guard smacked him on the head with the butt of the gun, then grabbed Joshua's sleeve, pulled him into the barracks, and went through all of his belongings. He took nearly every piece of clothing Joshua owned, then made him write a statement saying he'd gladly donated the clothes to local people who'd lost their belongings in Allied air raids. The guard led Joshua back outside to wait for his turn to be questioned. Since crossing into Transylvania, his magic picture of the general had lost its powers.

In the end, a group of Romanians was found responsible for the sabotage. They were shipped out of the camp, no one knew to where.

Joshua was initially assigned to build the prefabricated barracks, but was soon transferred to a team constructing a new kitchen for the mill workers. When it was nearly finished, the Swiss manager of the plant, who was a civilian, asked the kitchen crew if any of them could build a crib, since he was expecting visitors who had a baby. Joshua, as had become his habit, volunteered. Grateful to be crafting something upon which he could flex his creative skills, and happy to spend as much time doing it as possible, he lathed and routed, sanded and etched, notched and joined, completely absorbed in his work. Of sturdy design yet with intricate decorative flourishes, even the pickiest parent would've been pleased to see their child sleeping in this crib. Delighted, the mill manager was inspired to set up a wood shop for Joshua and a buddy of his, where they built things for use around camp, from tables and chairs to ladders to picture frames for the manager's house.

The manager became Joshua's supervisor, and also his friend. He would often invite Joshua to his house, ostensibly to consult on projects, though they would usually end up drinking tea around the kitchen table and listening to BBC Radio. Joshua, naturally, followed the progress of the war, and faithfully reported the news to the rest of his company. Each bulletin was heartening, as the Russians continued to push the Germans back, and the other Allies had begun to inch their way across France. Joshua kept his ears tuned for even the smallest bit of information about the Jews deported from Subcarpathia, but he learned nothing.

So accustomed to being treated as an equal, Joshua sometimes forgot that he was, in fact, a slave. After one enjoyable hour spent with the plant manager, Joshua took his leave with half a cheese Danish still in his hand, eating complacently as he strolled back to his workshop. Before he got there, he was spotted by the camp lieutenant—an ogre who relished any excuse to punish the laborers—who called the guards down upon this Jew and his contraband pastry. For his crime, Joshua was sentenced to hang by his wrists, which were tied behind his back, from a tree branch. The punishment was approved by Hungarian military code, as long as the guilty man was not actually pulled into the air. The camp commander, who observed, made sure that the tips of Joshua's toes still touched the ground. He hung there for half an hour before being cut down, by which time his torqued and tender arms felt a few inches longer and his shoulders seemed on the verge of popping from their sockets.

Very few of the barracks that the Jewish laborers were building ever got completed. The windows were supposed to be assembled in a nearby camp for Russian POWs, but the workers there were intentionally clumsy and kept breaking the glass. Before long, there was a backlog of partially finished buildings that were never shipped anywhere, spread out in the fields around the mill like a newly built ghost town. While discipline remained strict, there was little sense of urgency around filling the German army's demands. Even the camp's officers were halfhearted, since it was no secret that the war would soon be lost.

A German Luftwaffe captain named Werner, whose air base was nearby and who had requested some of the new barracks for his men, stopped by regularly to check on his order. Surprisingly, he mingled among the Jews, treated them with respect, and even became friendly with them. Once, when a horse stabled at the air base was injured, then shot, the German brought half of its meat to Joshua's company, thinking the Jews would be hungry and want to eat it. Although they *were* hungry—with only half a loaf of bread, plus two bowls of pea soup each day—they weren't desperate enough to eat an animal that none thought was fit for consumption. Not wanting to offend, however, they accepted the meat and then buried it.

As months passed and the air base still hadn't received the barracks it needed, the Luftwaffe captain came to the mill one day and chewed out the plant manager and the camp commander. On his way toward the exit gate, a laborer who'd overheard him felt comfortable enough to say, "Werner, you already lost the war. Why are you getting so upset?" Werner just shook his head and chuckled. "I know, I know. So what can I do?"

Throughout the spring and summer of 1944, voices within the Romanian government, including King Michael's, urged Antonescu to sign an armistice with Stalin. The Soviets had already captured all of Northern Bukovina and Transnistria, including Odessa. At any moment, they could cross into Romania, after which the Romanians would be powerless to negotiate peace terms. But on August 5, Antonescu met with Hitler and assured the Führer that he wasn't going to abandon him. "I could not and would not, even if I lived a million years," Antonescu later explained, "stab a comrade in the back who had been alongside me in an action."

Convinced of Antonescu's intractability and the damage it would wreak, King Michael led a coup on August 23. Antonescu was arrested and his government dismissed. The Soviet army pressed forward, as Stalin wanted to dictate the terms of any truce. German forces trying to hold the line were routed, and Romanian army units collapsed, some refusing to fight. The first Russian tanks rumbled into Bucharest on August 30, and an armistice was signed twelve days later. Before long, the Romanian army was fighting on the side of the Allies, and Soviet troops moved freely throughout the country.

Sensing that the end was looming, the deportation of Hungarian Jews was accelerated. Even Jewish labor units were beginning to be liquidated. Eichmann was racing the clock to complete his grisly task.

⸺⸺⸺

Joshua's unit got the order to move out sometime in late September. Since the nearby railway lines had been bombed, they were forced to march for over a week to a train station many miles to the west. They were being moved away from the front, they were told, for their safety.

The squad of some 250 Jewish laborers was led by one officer and escorted by ten guards. The officer, a Romanian national, had left his uniform behind and wore civilian clothes, so he could more easily escape if the Russians caught up to them. The men cut across the broad Crisul Repede valley, then headed west, from hamlet to hamlet, along the base of the Apuseni Mountains. During the first day, trudging along through dismal morning showers and into a steamy Indian summer afternoon, Joshua threw away his suitcase. Most of his clothing had been confiscated months earlier, so he owned little more than what he was wearing anyway. He tied his blanket over his shoulder and tucked a large envelope—filled with the documents and photos that his father had sent him, along with the two watches—inside his shirt. The unit slept that night in a pasture on the edge of a small village.

The following day, while marching along a path between villages, the labor company encountered a Romanian forest ranger. The ranger asked one of the Hungarian guards who was in charge, and they pointed to the captain. As the two Romanians talked between themselves, the laborers walked on, thinking the captain was simply engaged in friendly conversation. But that night, as they made camp in a field, the captain pulled aside the camp's Jewish Council, which had been responsible for fairly distributing any food and clothing that had managed to make its way to the mill from Jewish aid agencies. Joshua was the council secretary, while the camp cook was president.

The captain told the council what the ranger they'd met on the trail that day had said: The Jews were not being repositioned, but instead were being shipped to certain death and had better escape if they valued their lives. Though the captain himself wasn't aware of these plans—he was just ordered to get them to the train—the ranger had been so certain, so convincing, that the captain had believed him.

"I'll give you one chance to do what you will," he said. "Tonight I'm going to visit friends in the village up ahead. The guards will be staying here, and they will have guns. But all of the ammunition is locked up in boxes, and I have the only key. I'll be sure to take it with me. The ranger swore that the Romanians who live in the mountains hate the Hungarians, and would gladly help you to spite them. That's the best I can offer you. Good luck with whatever you decide to do. Now get back to your people."

The council members talked among themselves, debating whether this could possibly be true. Joshua tended to believe it. A few months earlier, before the tracks had been bombed, he'd seen a train of cattle cars pass the sawmill; from a distance, he thought he heard the mooing of cows inside, but when it rolled by, he realized it was people moaning inside the cars. They were crying for water, their hands straining through the small grated windows. He still hadn't heard of the death camps, not even on the BBC, and it never occurred to him to conclude that that's where the train he saw was bound. But now, with the warning of the ranger, it seemed plausible. And even if it wasn't true, escaping sounded like a good idea; maybe, Joshua thought, he'd be able to join a group of Czech partisans and fight against the Nazis himself.

The council members spread the word among the other men in their company. Some were convinced; others weren't, but were eager to escape regardless; and still others thought it was preposterous, and that they had a better chance of riding out the war with their unit than by abandoning it. Among the last group were about fifty religious Jews who were certain that God would take care of them. ("Unfortunately," my grandfather told me, "He didn't.")

That evening, when the company retired, many feigned sleep. Just after midnight, in groups of about ten at a time, they silently slipped out of camp and into the forest behind them. Almost to a man, those who stayed behind were murdered in concentration camps.

The deserters scattered through the Apuseni Mountains. Joshua and his handful of companions hiked southeast, toward the heart of the range, where they felt their chances of hiding from the Hungarians sure to hunt them would be most successful. Though neither as vast nor rugged as the Carpathians further east, the Apuseni was a snarl of forests, canyons, and caverns, at relatively low altitudes, which was important with winter weather a month away.

For the first few days after their getaway, Joshua and his friends avoided the dirt roads that connected the many villages scattered among the hills. Instead, they meandered through a maze of tight, stream-carved gorges, and up and down slopes so steep that every step was a battle with gravity. The ascents were breathtakingly strenuous, while each descent demanded stiff resistance against the momentum that sought to peel them off the mountainsides. A thick canopy of leaves blocked the sky, filtering the light into an eerie greenish-gray. A cushion of dead leaves fallen in years past filled the air with the pungent odor of decay, and crunched loudly beneath every footstep, making the men nervous. Their clothes were perpetually damp, either from sweat or the rains that fell intermittently. They slept in caves, hundreds of which pock the Apuseni's limestone core.

After a few days, hunger forced them to seek refuge in a village. They had no idea where they were, so when they came across a road, they simply followed it uphill, deeper into the mountains. They emerged from the forest into a rolling meadow that fanned out like an amphitheater, ringed by a grassy, horseshoe-shaped ridge. Huge haystacks speckled the basin, and herds of shaggy sheep browsed along the hillsides, sticking so closely together that from a distance, each flock looked like one giant white organism with hundreds of little black legs. Lined with prickly purple thistle and mint so potent that the men could taste it with every breath, the road led to a hamlet of some thirty homes. Some were made of mud brick, others of thick, rough cut planks, notched in the corners and fitted together atop stone foundations. Some were painted in bright pastels, like rose or turquoise; others weren't plastered at all. Their pitched roofs, covered with chipped terra-cotta tiles, overhung small wooden porches.

Unsure of the reception they'd receive, the fugitives approached a woman hanging laundry over the fence surrounding her courtyard. She spoke some Hungarian, and Joshua explained their situation to her. "I think we can help, but I need to speak to the others first," the woman replied.

The people of the Apuseni had neither a great love nor a great hatred for Jews, but they were famous throughout Romania for waging a guerrilla-type rebellion that drove out Hungarian rulers in the nineteenth century, and they'd resented the return of their old enemies. What's more, a large number of men from the area had been abducted into the Hungarian labor corps, winning few friends for Hungary among the locals. The villagers also feared that they might be viewed by the approaching Soviets as Axis collaborators, and that helping the Jews—who were thought to be friends of Russia—would prove that they had no allegiance to Hungary whatsoever. Together, the villagers agreed to shelter Joshua and the others until it was safe for them to leave the mountains.

The Jews were separated and assigned to different households. The peasants, among whom traditions of hospitality ran deep, gave the runaway laborers their beds and laid blankets on the floor for themselves. In return, Joshua and his friends helped their hosts prepare for winter, for which the villagers were grateful, since most of the men had either been taken away by the Hungarians or were off tending sheep in the hills, keeping them in the high meadows longer than usual, trying to stay out of sight.

Joshua sat on a stump in the field behind his hideout, shucking heaps of corn, then laying the golden ears out to dry. A few chickens and geese strutted around, inspecting his work; a cat prowled in the squash patch, hunting. Beside him sat the woman with whom he was staying, whose name was Berta, like his mother's. She was in her twenties and beautiful, with full cheeks permanently blushed by the rough affections of the sun and wind. Her hands, with powerful fingers the texture of unpeeled carrots, looked twice as old as her face. She spoke only a few words of Hungarian, just enough to convey the necessities and make small talk. Mostly, they communicated with their eyes.

Together they chopped wood and arranged it into neat rectangular piles, Berta showing Joshua how to lay each row of logs at a right angle to the one below it, endowing the stack with structural stability as it rose to shoulder height. In the garden, they plucked bean pods from man-high stalks sprouting green, spade-shaped leaves; from the fruit trees along the fence they picked plums, then stored them in a wooden vat to ferment. They walked half a mile down the creek to a walnut grove, where Joshua shook tree branches with a long, straight pole and Berta gathered the nuts that fell to the ground, depositing them into a woven basket. Stealing glances at her as she bent over, Joshua couldn't help but wonder what it would be like to settle in this village, and whether Berta would convert.

It might have been blissful, except for the Hungarian patrols that kept them on edge. A few times that first week, Joshua and his friends were sent scattering into the forest as soldiers knocked on the villagers' doors. They remained hidden, behind bushes or buried under leaves, until children, shouting "Friends, friends," were sent to tell them the coast was clear. Sensing it was too dangerous for them to remain there, the peasants decided to hide the Jews higher in the mountains, well off the road, at their shepherd cabins. These primitive, one-room huts were made from the stones that were scattered across the treeless slopes on which they perched. Shepherds, dressed in long sheepskin coats, occasionally passed with their flocks, driving them along with the help of a few intimidating dogs and shouts of "Yo ho!" But the fugitives' most frequent visitors were the women from the village, who hauled up bread and buckets of bean soup every day—a welcome break from peas. There wasn't much to do up on the hillside but wait. At least from the cabins they had expansive views of the mountains, which were too low and gentle to inspire awe, but were pretty enough to be soothing. Joshua would sit outside his hut, gaze at the scenery, and allow himself to be overtaken by moments of peace.

Usually, though, a current of impatience coursed through him. He was agitated by unknowing, and he knew nothing about anything that mattered. He laid no bets on whether he'd make it out of the mountains before being caught, and had no idea if he'd ever see his family again. At last, a few weeks later and a few days after the first snow flurries fell, word reached the village that Soviet forces had captured most of Transylvania. Joshua and his friends were brought down from the cabins and sent south with a shepherd, who led them for three days through the mountains, taking them behind Soviet lines. They no longer had to fear being sent to a German concentration camp, but did face the possibility of being detained and sent to a Soviet work camp.

Atop a ridge cloaked in stratus, the guide pointed to a goat trail and told them to follow it into a town that sat far below. Then he turned in the direction whence they had come and was quickly swallowed by the fog. The trail snaked down the flank of a sharply cut valley, then crisscrossed a creek that somersaulted along the bottom of the gorge. Long clouds, like gray fox tails, hung low between the heavily wooded slopes. A light drizzle fell. Between the fog and the forest, it was impossible to see more than fifty meters ahead. Soon, the men found themselves splashing along a rutted muddy track.

They came to a clearing where they saw a Russian tank sitting outside a peasant's house. Any fears of being taken prisoner and deported to Siberia, as Joshua knew had happened to some Jewish labor units, vanished from his mind; he couldn't resist the urge to run to the soldiers, throw his arms around them, and thank them for liberating him. But when he and the others approached the house, they heard arguing. They peered in through a window and spied two Russian soldiers fighting over a shirt the peasant had left behind.

"Give it to me or I'll kill you!" one of them yelled, waving a pistol, and Joshua quietly whispered, "Let's get out of here." Through his head flashed an old joke about a Russian who had gone bear hunting and, after a fruitless day, came across a Jew in the forest, whom he decided to shoot instead. When the Jew protested, the Russian answered, "Prove to me you're not a bear." In other words, any excuse was good enough to kill a Jew, and Joshua didn't want to take any chances with soldiers who were ready to murder one another over a piece of clothing. Their sudden joy at encountering the Russians retreated behind a wary vigilance.

Following the creek, the dirt track brought them into a small town at the valley's mouth, along a main road. It was surrounded by livestock pastures and cornfields, and its centerpiece was an old wooden church. The streets teemed with Soviet soldiers. The small band of soggy runaways hoped they might appear inconspicuous, but after weeks of hiding and days of trekking through the mountains, this was impossible. They walked unmolested for about a hundred meters before arriving at the intersection with the town's main street. There, they were confronted by a tank. As if the machine itself noticed them, the turret turned until its big gun stared them in the face. They froze.

To run amid all these soldiers would be as sensible as yelling, "I hate Stalin!" Staying where they were might prove no smarter. The lid of the tank banged open, and an officer popped his head out. "Surround them!" he ordered five soldiers standing nearby. In an instant, their rifles were drawn and trained on their nervous targets.

"We're screwed," Joshua muttered to his cohorts, as the officer climbed down from the tank.

"No we're not!" said one of his friends. "I know that guy!"

"Did you leave your brain in the mountains? How can you possibly know him?" Joshua asked incredulously. His friend didn't answer, instead shouting to the officer, "Itzik! Itzik!" The officer, his face registering complete surprise, turned to the Jew who had called his name. Then he smiled, ran to him, and embraced him. The officer, it turned out, was a Hungarian Jew by birth, and had attended a yeshiva with Joshua's companion. Years earlier, he'd been assigned to a labor unit on the Russian front, and had been sent across a minefield ahead of a Hungarian combat unit. Miraculously, he'd made it across Soviet lines without tripping any mines or being gunned down by the Russians, and he immediately joined the Red Army. Since then, he'd risen to the rank of lieutenant.

Itzik dismissed his soldiers, then ushered the fugitives into a general store, which had a few tables and chairs set up near a woodstove, and almost nothing on the shelves hanging behind the counter. The lieutenant poured them each a shot of vodka from a silver flask as he listened to the story of their escape—and heard for the first time about the deportation of Hungarian Jews. When they were through, he promised to help them, and told them to wait in the shop and dry off while he tried to arrange a few things. Joshua and the others stood around the stove, fantasizing about what they would do next, mocking each others' frightened reactions to the Russians, and laughing, giddy at their improbable deliverance and their first tangible sense that the course of the war was irreversible.

Itzik came back about an hour or so later with a small truck, the bed of which was covered with a drab canvas canopy, and drove the happy men to Oradea, a city to the north that had been liberated from the Hungarians a few days earlier—and not far from the sawmill where they'd once worked. There, Itzik consulted with a fellow Soviet officer, then drove to a house hurriedly vacated by a

Hungarian captain. In one of the closets hung a rack of Hungarian army summer uniforms, which Joshua and his buddies changed into after ripping the insignias off. Itzik told them they could stay there for a few days if they needed to. He had to be getting back to the village himself, so he wrote them a note, saying they were to be granted free passage through the occupied zone—which might or might not be effective, he said, but better to have it than not.

A few Russian soldiers were also living in the house, and Joshua gave them the two watches sent to him by his father—which weren't worth much—for food money and protection for himself and his friends, along with the promise of a ride to Arad. This city, a few hours to the south, would be the best possible place for them to orient themselves to their new reality as free and homeless men; Arad's Jewish community had remained relatively intact throughout the war, since neither Germans nor Hungarians had set foot there.

Upon being deposited at the edge of Arad, they asked directions to the synagogue and walked through the heart of the city, past the regal city hall—built of white stone, with long rows of windows, columns, and arched entryways—and through a grassy park bordered by colorfully plastered buildings, whose doorways and windows were topped with carved lintels, many of whose facades were adorned with sculpted reliefs. On a side street a few blocks away, they found the temple. It was a two-story brick building, plastered in light ochre tones. Just below the peaked roofline, inside the triangular pediment, was a carved rendering of the Ten Commandments; atop each of the plain columns between the windows, a Star of David was etched. Joshua's crew was sure they'd find people there willing to take them in, but though they were fed, no one invited them home. They spent the night sleeping on the hard synagogue benches.

The following morning they went to the Jewish community center, the nexus for information and aid to Jewish refugees. A number of other Hungarian labor servicemen who had escaped from their units were there, most of whom had been stationed in Yugoslavia. Joshua was speaking with one who'd been in town for a week, when he overheard a woman's voice asking if anyone happened to be from Uzhgorod. He quickly excused himself and approached the woman, introducing himself. In less than a minute, Joshua realized that he was talking to the sister of one of Bela's best friends. The man occasionally contributed editorials to *Zsido Neplap* and was, my grandfather recalled, "the biggest *schlemiel* in town—he knew everything but how to earn a penny." But his sister seemed sharp, and she and her husband invited Joshua home with them. They were poor and could only take him, so Joshua bid a happy farewell to his companions and went with these strangers, who felt like extended family. They'd received no word from their family in Uzhgorod since early spring, and couldn't offer Joshua any information about the fate of the deportees. They did tell him that there was a community of Czech refugees in Bucharest, and that his best bet to join the partisans was to go to the Romanian capital and try to find out if such a thing was possible. Since he had no money, they gave him a few coins the next morning and wished him good luck as he headed to the train station.

What they'd given him wasn't enough for the fare to Bucharest, so when Joshua boarded the train, he gave everything he had to the conductor, pleading to be allowed to ride to the end of the line. The conductor relented, and by evening Joshua had reached his destination. He stepped off the train and onto the platform, and paused for a second to get his bearings before being swept up in the river of people coursing by in hats and heavy coats, carrying suitcases. In that brief instant, he heard someone shouting his name. *There must be someone else on the train named Joshua*, he thought. Certainly, no one could be calling for him. But a moment later, a man came running up and threw his arms around my grandfather's neck.

"Joshua! I'm so glad to see you!" the man said. Joshua didn't recognize him at first, and his face must have conveyed his confusion.

"It's me, Jakob! Don't you remember? We were in Betar summer camp together in Uzhgorod!"

Joshua's memory was jogged, and he greeted his old friend with an incredulous smile. "What are you doing here?" Joshua asked.

Jakob replied that he'd come to take a train to the coast, but his business wasn't urgent and he could catch the next one; it was more important to reconnect with an old friend. Jakob led Joshua to a coffee shop just outside the station where they sat and talked. Jakob had also heard nothing about the Jews deported from Uzhgorod, but he wasn't optimistic, saying there'd been rumors about death camps, and he preferred to believe the worst rather than nurse false hopes. He couldn't give Joshua a place to stay, but told him how to find a small temple whose Hasidic rabbi opened the doors to refugees—even Zionists. Most Jews in Bucharest wouldn't lift a finger to aid their brethren, Jakob warned, but said that the Czech ex-pat colony would help him find a more permanent place to stay and make sure he could eat.

Jakob walked Joshua to the temple, gave him a note with an address and a message on it, and instructed him to give it to one of the boys who would come to study with the rabbi in the morning. The elderly bearded rabbi invited Joshua to sleep on the temple floor, and the next day Joshua gave the note to a boy, who ran off with it. Half an hour later, one of Jakob's friends arrived and took Joshua to an apartment where the leaders of the Czech community lived.

Though Bucharest wasn't in a combat zone for long, it had endured three intense air raids during the war, two by the Allies and one by the Germans. As Joshua made his way through the city, he saw the bombed-out remains of the city's neighborhoods and showpiece buildings, including the royal palace and the university. Many windows in churches and apartments had been shattered; some gaped with toothy shards of glass still hanging in them, while others had been boarded up. The walls of building after building were scarred by bullet holes from the brief urban battles fought between Romanian and German forces, after the Romanian armistice with the Soviets was announced. More than the structural damage to the city, however, Joshua was struck by the profusion of unkempt beggars and crippled men in battered uniforms who seemed to have nowhere to go and nothing to do.

When Joshua arrived at the Czechs' headquarters, he showed a man his identity papers and was welcomed into a sparsely furnished studio apartment with three beds, a few hard wooden chairs, and a large table piled with documents. He told his story for the third time in three days. He mentioned that Jakob had said there were rumors of Nazi death camps, and asked if there was anything to them. The man told Joshua of Vrba's Auschwitz report from some eight months earlier; no one knew if it was true, the man said, but it was so detailed that it would have required a feat of twisted imagination to invent. Joshua fell silent for a moment, then asked about joining the underground Czech army, of which he'd also heard rumors. The man told him to forget it—there was no reliable way to find the partisans, especially with the front lines as fluid as they were.

"Well, what am I supposed to do?" Joshua asked in exasperation.

"Stay here in Bucharest for a while, and try to be patient," the man replied. "This war won't last forever, and you might be able to get home before too long." Uzhgorod had just been taken by the Soviets, the man said, but the situation was brittle and the city too vulnerable to return to yet. The man then asked Jakob's friend to take Joshua to a house where Czech refugees lodged and ate for free, knowing that Joshua had no money or valuables left to trade.

The house was two stories high, and very comfortably appointed. The living room boasted a plush couch and two leather chairs, and in the dining room was a polished table of solid oak. The glass cabinets were filled with china. Over the fireplace was a stone mantle with horses' heads hewn on both ends. Upon it, and hanging on the walls throughout the house, were framed photographs of a handsome, serious-looking Nazi SS officer. The woman who lived there was his wife. She was German and in her mid-forties, and was pretty despite the stress that creased her face and painted dark circles under her eyes.

Her husband had been stationed in Bucharest as a military attaché, and they had lived there together for a couple of years. At the end of August, he'd retreated with the German army, but left her behind, where he felt she'd be safe. She had no idea whether or not he was alive. As the Russians occupied the city, she struck a deal with the Czech community: They'd give her false Czech identification papers to conceal her true nationality if she would open her home to Czech refugees. She didn't mind if her guests were Jewish; the war had obliterated any ideology she might have had, and she now sympathized with her boarders simply as human beings whose lives had been torn apart.

For a couple of weeks, Joshua roomed on the second floor. Impatient to be doing something, anything, instead of just waiting for the war to end, he sought out the Zionist organizations operating in the city and put himself at their disposal, volunteering in their offices whenever they asked. They were well aware of his father's reputation, and quickly saw that Joshua embodied the same commitment to the cause that they knew Bela had. At the end of November, they informed him that a boat was preparing to sail for Istanbul full of immigrants heading to Palestine, and, thanks to his impeccable Zionist pedigree, they asked him to join the crew and take charge of all passenger-related issues. Joshua seized the invitation. He was certain that if his family survived the war, they'd soon make their way to Palestine themselves, and he felt he could be of more use to his people there than in Romania.

A few days later, he boarded a train for the port city of Constanta, still wearing the Hungarian army summer uniform he'd been given in Oradea.

THIRTY-THREE

In Constanta, Joshua and a crew of help-
ers made sure that each of the long bunks
installed in the cargo hold would support the weight of
hundreds of bodies. First-aid supplies were loaded onto the
ship. Enough drinking water was taken on board to last 600
people for fourteen days—in case of any delays—along
with food, which consisted of salami, cheese, bread, and
halvah. In storing the food, Joshua made his one big mistake: In a pantry barely large enough to hold everything,
he packed all the salami, then all the cheese, then all the
bread, then all the halvah. In order to get to the bread and
cheese, the refugees had to eat their way to it, and by the
end of the first day, people were vomiting up halvah all
over the boat.

Sailing from Constanta to Istanbul was not a casual
undertaking. Almost exactly three years earlier, the
Struma, a seventy-four-year-old, fifty-foot-long vessel,
left Constanta for Palestine. After sputtering into Istanbul
crippled by mechanical failure, it was towed back into the
Black Sea, where it was torpedoed by a Soviet submarine—
allegedly as a favor to their new British allies. Only one of
the 760-plus passengers survived the attack. As a result of
the global attention this aroused, as well as the obviously

tragic condition of European Jewry in the 1940s, the British loos-
ened their immigration policies a notch, allowing a few thousand
Jews each year who could make it to Istanbul into Palestine. But
the risks were still high; on August 5, 1944, four months before
the *Toros* sailed from Constanta with Joshua and Isadora aboard, the
Mefkure was blown up in the Black Sea by another Soviet submarine.
Those who survived the sinking were machine-gunned in the water
as they clung to floating wreckage.

These maritime refugee missions were carried out by a complex partnership between Jewish agencies in Palestine, Romania,
and Turkey, the governments of Turkey and Romania, and maverick
Gentile entrepreneurs, mostly from Greece and Bulgaria. Old boats
were hired and bureaucratic red tape was cut with bribes. Little, of
course, could be done to reduce the risks of storms, floating mines,
or hostile submarines and airplanes—both Russian and German.
But Jews clamored to attempt the passage nonetheless.

Joshua felt more alive than he had in a long time. Rather than
working—or trying to avoid working—for the Hungarian army, he
was once again immersed in the cause that had been so central to his
existence since the day he was born. With nothing he could do to
directly help his own family, this was the next best thing. He knew
that if his father could see him, his eyes would twinkle with pride.

Pandemonium consumed departure day. One thousand Jews
had arrived expecting to board, when there were places for only
six hundred. Heated discussions among the leadership ensued over
which groups to leave behind, while throngs of agitated refugees
swarmed the port, indignant and afraid of possibly being forsaken
on this freezing winter day. In the end, the leadership committee
decided to take everyone. If all went well, they'd be in Istanbul

in a couple of days, and the overcrowding would be a temporary inconvenience inflicted upon people who knew all about enduring far worse.

As they shuffled up the gangplank, Joshua selected people to pose as war wounded, pulling them aside so his crew could bandage them up and arrange them on deck. A respectable facsimile of a Red Cross flag was already atop the mast, snapping in the wind. Once the boat was at sea, a yellow quarantine flag would also be raised. The ship's disguise, it was hoped, would convince enemy planes and ships that the *Toros* was on a sanctioned aid mission, rather than carrying Jews. While most of the refugees were orderly and compliant, others were boisterous and unruly. Reports came to Joshua of people who'd been pickpocketed or had their belongings stolen, and a few fights had to be quelled.

As he was trying to manage the mass of human cargo, Joshua was told by the ship's captain—a Bulgarian—that the boat was taking on water, and something had to be done quickly. Since the metal sheathing on the hull's exterior had been stripped off for fear it would attract magnetic floating mines, the seams between the wooden planks below the waterline became dangerously porous. Without alerting the passengers, he and his crew ripped up spare blankets, located and triaged the leaks, then stuffed them with the rags in order of their severity. Meanwhile, the ship was gradually being covered in regurgitated halvah. Hardly a minute went by without someone approaching Joshua with a problem or a question. By early evening, his brain felt ready to burst. He asked one of his friends to wake him in fifteen minutes, then crawled under the canvas covering of one of the few lifeboats on board, and passed out. It was the only place he could get a moment of peace.

At night, once everyone was supposed to be asleep in the cargo hold and Joshua expected he'd finally be able to get some rest, he decided to make one last survey of the ship, from bow to stern, to ensure that all was well. Near the back of the boat, he found a terrified young woman weeping on deck. Something about her—maybe her vulnerability, maybe her tears or the imploring dark eyes that shed them—penetrated through his exhaustion. Here was a real person, not an anonymous face among a thousand others. She was in distress and, he couldn't help thinking, beautiful. He was moved to take care of her that night.

After enduring the night on deck, after their ludicrous, translated engagement the next morning, Isadora saw Joshua only in passing, but always with a smile of acknowledgment on his face, as he walked the ship, inspecting conditions and solving problems with a natural authority.

In the evening, as the *Toros* approached Istanbul, it was met and towed in by a Turkish coast guard vessel whose crew had been paid off to safely escort the ship. It docked that night at the port on the city's European side. The lights in the harbor shimmered in the black mirror of the water. The air was calm, the clear sky aswirl with stars. Though they all knew they might encounter some insurmountable hurdle before reaching Palestine, a mood of muted celebration settled over the refugees. Joshua found Isadora and Yisrael, and brought them to the officers' cabin, where a dozen men sat on cots or on the floor, discussing logistics for the following day. There, they slept on the floor.

Word came in the morning that the British would honor their agreement and allow the refugees to enter Palestine. Six long tables manned by British consular officials were set up on shore by the end of the gangplank. There, they recorded the name and birth date of each passenger, creating one common visa for all. To maintain some pretense of order, the refugees were sent off the ship in groups— all Czech citizens together, all Romanians together, all orphans together, and the like. Isadora didn't expect to see much of Joshua again. While waiting in line, the Jews were served sandwiches and water by Turkish soldiers. With the visa completed, everyone boarded the *Toros* again to be ferried over to Istanbul's Asian side. Despite the best-laid plans of Joshua and his compatriots, even the pretense of order evaporated once they got there.

An eager mass of people stampeded from the boat to the waiting train. Isadora and Yisrael became separated in the confusion. When she got to the station, she stood by the train, her head turning from side to side as if she was a human lighthouse, searching for her brother. But there were just too many people. She gave up, figuring she'd have a better chance of finding him on board. Grabbing the handrail, she climbed the metal steps into a car in the middle of the train, turned right, and walked from car to car, looking for Yisrael in each compartment.

The train was clean and well maintained. Each compartment was outfitted with two upholstered benches facing each other, a large window in between, and luggage racks above. By the time Isadora reached the lead car, the alleyways and minarets of Istanbul were slowly slipping by outside. She hadn't found her brother yet, but in one of the first compartments she accidentally found Joshua. He motioned for her to take a place beside him on his already-full bench, and moved over a few inches to make room for her by the window. Through an interpreter, she said she had to look for her brother and couldn't stay; he asked her to come back with Yisrael once they were reunited, and she did.

The train chugged south across the Turkish countryside, through pine forests, up valleys cradled between snowy mountain peaks that gleamed like massive domes of salt, and out across snow-covered steppes. For the first day on the rails, Joshua and Isadora hardly spoke, since they had no language in common. But a feeling of togetherness was communicated without words. Joshua had told the others in their compartment about their mock engagement on the *Toros*, so everyone began jokingly referring to them as husband and wife. On the second day, a young rabbi who sat on the bench opposite Joshua said to him, "You know, if you do want to marry her, I'll be happy to perform the ceremony."

Joshua's eyes widened at the rabbi's offer. But he allowed himself to consider it. He looked at Isadora, then back to the rabbi, and said, "Okay."

The interpreter translated Joshua's marriage proposal and Isadora burst out laughing. She'd never heard anything so ridiculous. But she looked at Joshua, knew deep down that he was as kind a man as she ever hoped to meet, and agreed, with one condition: that everyone leave the compartment but for herself, her fiancée, and the rabbi. She knew what she was doing was rash, and, she later said, "I didn't want anyone to see how crazy I am."

But privacy wasn't an option, she was told. There had to be ten men there to make a minyan. With a shrug, she consented.

Meanwhile, Yisrael couldn't believe what was happening. He urged his sister to come to her senses. "Are you nuts?! You have no idea who this guy is!" he stressed. "He's a total stranger. He could be insane or violent or already married. You can't even speak to him!"

"You're absolutely right," Isadora answered, then started laughing again. "But really, why not?"

The rabbi produced an old black-and-white prayer shawl and tied it above them from one luggage rack to the other, improvising the ritual wedding canopy. Instead of a long white dress and fancy shoes, Isadora wore a pair of scuffed hiking boots over knee-high socks, a brown tweed skirt, and a rust-colored sweater she had knitted for herself at the orphanage. She borrowed a scarf from another woman to use as a veil. Joshua wore the Hungarian summer uni-form—still just about all he owned—over a black turtleneck. They had no rings, so one of their witnesses gave them each a small coin to exchange instead. The rabbi handwrote a *ketuba*—the traditional Jewish wedding contract—on a piece of paper with a hand shaken by the motion of the train. In the place where the location of the wedding is noted, he wrote, "between Konya and Adana."

Word of the wedding had spread throughout the car, and people crammed together by the open door of Joshua and Isadora's com-partment, jostling for a glimpse of the ceremony, as though they craved some proof that life could yet bestow spontaneous bless-ings. The ritual was short and simple. There was no room for the bride to circle the groom seven times; there was no glass to stomp on. They exchanged vows over metallic clacking and creaking, and Joshua gave Isadora a first, tentative kiss—on the forehead. Isadora laughed once more.

Now actually husband and wife, Joshua and Isadora still couldn't talk to each other, but they held hands and gazed at one another, speaking with their eyes, slight movements of their lips, the angles at which they held their heads. Something blossomed in their silence. They'd have to wait a year, until Isadora learned Hebrew, before they could really communicate; my grandmother likes to say that it was the happiest year of their marriage.

When I asked my grandparents if they had any idea what they were getting into at the time, my grandfather answered, "We were alone. I had nobody; she had only her brother. I felt it was better to be with somebody, and I think she felt the same."

"Actually," my grandmother interrupted, "I really didn't realize what I was doing."

The refugees changed to a French-run train at the Syrian border, and in Beirut, they transferred to a British train. Unlike those they'd ridden so far, this last was composed of cattle cars. A number of the refugees panicked at the prospect of being loaded into them, but the cars weren't overcrowded and the doors were kept open. What's more, before it pulled out of the station, members of the Jewish Agency placed sacks of ripe oranges in each car. Many of the passengers had never eaten one before; with the first bite, they tasted the promise of a new, sweet life. The arid, rocky landscape they traversed was starkly beautiful, and unlike anything Joshua or Isadora had ever seen. As the train clattered down the coast under bright sapphire skies, the lapis Mediterranean crashed in white waves to the west, while green fields and orchards rolled by to the east. Joshua and Isadora were both filled with the sense that they were exactly where they were meant to be. It was the closest thing to a honeymoon they could have, and as far from where they'd come as they could imagine.

THIRTY-FOUR

Their vision of paradise didn't last long. After arriving in Haifa, Joshua and Isadora's first stop, along with everyone else on their train, was the refugee camp at Atlit. Ringed by barbed wire, canvas tents covered the dry, pebbly grounds. Inside the tents they found metal cots with straw mattresses, and nothing else. Men and women slept in separate areas of the camp, but were allowed to socialize during the day. Normally used by the British to hold illegal immigrants indefinitely, for these legal immigrants, Atlit was a temporary quarantine facility. After two weeks, they were released.

Few, however, had anywhere to go, and little money to go there with. Recruiters from *kibbutzim* canvassed the refugee camp, inviting the immigrants to join their collective farms. Joshua had no interest in going to a kibbutz, since they were the domain of the Labor Zionists, and he was a Revisionist; besides, he had a useful trade, and believed he would quickly find work. Yisrael, however, who had no political loyalties, decided that living on a kibbutz sounded like a better way to begin life in a new land than tagging along with his sister and her new husband. He and Isadora said a teary good-bye, promising to see each other soon.

Joshua had spoken with a representative of the Revisionist Party who had visited the camp, wanting to know what kind of housing the party had prepared for the immigrants. There wasn't much, he was told. Since the start of World War II, new construction had virtually come to a standstill. There wasn't even enough housing for the Jews already in-country. Some were living in public shelters, others on the streets, some of whom would sleep overnight in empty bakery wagons until the bread was loaded into them in the early morning. The Revisionists did have a place where they could accommodate about a dozen people: the basement of a building under construction in Tel Aviv, which would later become their headquarters. Joshua and Isadora settled there with ten others.

At that time, Tel Aviv was bustling with over 165,000 people, three-quarters of whom had arrived from Europe in the 1930s. Automobile traffic filled streets lined with shops, restaurants, nightclubs, banks, and the occasional movie theater. Quality jazz combos played the best hotels. Some of the city's newest buildings were designed by Bauhaus architects who had fled Germany.

The groundwork for a viable nation had been laid throughout Jewish Palestine, which was known as the *Yishuv*. Haifa, in the north, had a large port on the Mediterranean; Tel Aviv had a smaller port of its own, as well as two nearby airports; electrical power plants had been built on the Jordan River; commercial potash production had begun along the Dead Sea. And, while the British colonial administration was still the ultimate authority in the land, the Yishuv was self-ruling in many regards. The Jewish Agency had been appointed to govern over the growth of the Jewish national home and appear as its face in the theater of international diplomacy. By 1937, one British report observed that the Agency "has created a complete administrative apparatus. This powerful and efficient organization amounts, in fact, to a Government existing side by side with the Mandatory [colonial] Government." Its chairman was David Ben-Gurion, leader of *Mapai*, the Socialist Zionist party.

While it didn't have the clout of Mapai, the Revisionist Party remained a potent opposition force in the life and politics of the Yishuv, most visibly with its *Irgun Tz'vai L'umi* (National Military Organization)—an armed security force first commanded by Vladimir Jabotinsky, which was the right-wing counterpart to the *Haganah*, the Jewish Agency's official militia.

Both Ben-Gurion and Jabotinsky were equally committed to the creation of an independent Israel and promoting Jewish immigration from Europe, legal or otherwise. That's about where their common ground ended. Ben-Gurion was a socialist, a capitalist; Ben-Gurion supported partitioning Palestine, as a concession to realism; Jabotinsky believed the Jews needed all of it, including Transjordan, which had already been promised to the Arabs. In response to Arab attacks on Jewish settlers, Ben-Gurion enforced a policy of restraint by the Haganah; Jabotinsky ordered swift and forceful retaliation by the Irgun. The competition between Labor Zionists and Revisionists to build the Jewish homeland according to their respective visions was intense and often antagonistic, fomenting a tension in the Yishuv that would take it to the precipice of civil war. After Arab resistance, this infighting was the greatest single threat to the future of a successful Jewish state. All in all, the Yishuv that Joshua and Isadora arrived in was a remarkable creation, but still in its adolescence, with major achievements to its credit and daunting problems to be solved.

While living in the basement of the building under construction, Joshua was introduced to a number of other Revisionists, some of whom had known his father. After about a week, one of Bela's old friends told Joshua of a radical housing scheme about to be hatched, and asked if Joshua wanted to be involved. Naturally, he did.

It had been learned that patients at a privately run mental hospital in the town of B'nai Barak, just outside of Tel Aviv, were being transferred to a public facility. Immigrants' groups had approached the asylum owners about leasing their soon-to-be-empty buildings as apartments, and the owners agreed. The rent they asked for, however, was astronomical. Since they wouldn't negotiate and it was impossible for nearly anyone in Palestine, let alone a bunch of poor refugees, to pay the asking price, the asylum was fated to be vacant as of Friday, December 29, 1944.

Around noon on that day, fifty-one hopeful immigrants climbed into the beds of two trucks in Tel Aviv and concealed themselves beneath canvas tarps, planning to occupy the facilities illegally. The trucks rolled out toward B'nai Barak and stopped on a small dirt road at the edge of an orchard, the far side of which bordered the asylum grounds. The orchard owner, who was in on the plan, escorted the immigrants through his property, encouraging them to pick all the fruit they could eat on the way. As the group neared the fence line, they were met by a small advance team, which had been scouting out the scene next door. The last of the patients had recently been taken away, they said, and just a couple of guards remained behind. This was their chance. The immigrants were divided into three units—one for each empty building—and were quietly ushered out the orchard's back gate and onto the asylum property.

Joshua, who had helped manage the truck transport much as he had the boat trip from Romania, now co-led a group of thirty—including Isadora—toward the main, two-story brick building. They strode quickly but calmly across a driveway and over a patch of grass. Just before they got to the door, they were intercepted by one of the guards. Blocking their way, he wanted to know what they thought they were doing. The group stopped, certain their plans were about to be foiled. But as soon as Joshua explained what was going on and why, the guard stepped to the side and opened the door, holding it ajar as the triumphant refugees bounded over the threshold.

Within minutes of the occupation, the people who lived in B'nai Barak began arriving at the asylum. Aside from their joy at receiving these Eastern European survivors into their community, the townspeople were thrilled to be rid of the mental institution; the words "B'nai Barak" had become slang for "nuthouse," the Yishuv's equivalent of "Bellevue," and its residents were eager to shed that reputation. One neighbor wheeled over a barrel of salted fish; a baker delivered a cart of fresh bread; local shops donated *matzah* and margarine; a few women brought pitchers of milk for the children, while another volunteered to organize her friends to wash all of the bed linens that had been left behind. Meanwhile, a three-man committee was formed from among the asylum's new tenants to handle all housing issues and disputes, with Joshua as its leader.

Once the food gifts were fairly distributed and people settled in, an Israeli flag was hung above the entry gate. The occupiers, along with a few hundred well-wishing onlookers, gathered beneath it and belted out "Hatikvah," the anthem of the Zionist movement, and later, the State of Israel.

As long as deep within the heart
A Jewish soul yearns
And forward, to the east,
An eye to Zion turns

Our hope is not yet lost,
The hope of two thousand years,
To be a free people in our land,
The land of Zion and Jerusalem.

Joshua's arm was wrapped tightly around Isadora's waist as he sang; she tried to hum along, even though she didn't know the words. Tears of emotion trickled down their cheeks and those of many others. For the first time, the refugees felt like they had truly found a home. By the end of the weekend, another seventy refugees had been welcomed into the asylum.

The occupation was the subject of articles, and even political cartoons, in Jewish newspapers including *Ha'aretz* and the *Palestine Post*. Since there were laws protecting squatters' rights, they couldn't just be booted out by the police, despite such efforts by a few of the asylum's owners. One of the owners, however, welcomed those who had taken over his building, sending over cakes as well as a crew that gave all the bedroom walls a coat of fresh paint. Within two weeks, thanks in part to the publicity their cause had generated, the immigrants worked out an arrangement with the landlords to pay a reasonable monthly rent.

In Joshua and Isadora's building, there was a shared kitchen on the ground floor, a few shared bathrooms, some dorm rooms with bunk beds, and a few private bedrooms. Since Joshua and Isadora were married, and since he carried the burden of being committee head, they were given a private room. Their first night in the asylum was their first night alone. When the door shut behind them and Joshua began to undress, Isadora became nervous. She knew nothing about being intimate with a man and was terrified of being seen naked.

"Since my father died when I was so young," my grandmother explained, "I didn't know there was anything more to being a wife than cooking and keeping house." They took things very slowly.

<hr />

Soon after Joshua's name was printed in articles about the asylum occupation, a steady stream of visitors who had been friends with his father dropped by to see him. One of them, by the name of Moshe Goldstein, told Joshua of a woodworking shop in Tel Aviv where craftspeople could rent space and machinery, and said he knew of a number of merchants who'd be glad to custom-order furniture from Joshua. Moshe also introduced Joshua to a pair of brothers who bought unfinished olive-wood jewelry boxes, bookends, and other trinkets from Arab woodworkers, then painted them and sold them to gift shops and British military PXs. Since the prevailing ethic of the time was to buy Jewish-made goods, the brothers told Joshua that if he could produce the items they needed for the same price as the Arabs, they'd give their business to him instead. Goldstein loaned Joshua some start-up money, and soon he was cutting and carving the olive wood he bought in Jerusalem's Old City, from a supplier named Ibrahim Attallah. The Arabs, my grandfather said, were the only ones who knew how to cure the wood so it wouldn't crack. ⟨══✕⟩

THIRTY-FIVE

While living at the mental asylum, Joshua secretly joined the Irgun, keeping even his new bride in the dark about his insurgent activities. It was his duty, he felt, to do whatever he could to help defend the Yishuv from Arab threats, and to bring about Israeli independence, especially for the Jews still in Europe, to whom Palestine's doors were shut. "More than ever, we needed a place in this world, and Israel was the only place in it that felt like ours," my grandfather explained. "We had talked to the British for thirty years. Immigration was virtually closed. There was nothing to talk about." By the time he entered the underground, Jabotinsky was dead, and the new commander of the Irgun was another former associate of his father, by the name of Menachem Begin.

Under Begin, the Irgun's primary mission had shifted from protecting Jews from Arab violence to forcibly kicking the British out of Palestine. A years-long ceasefire with the British in Palestine—called to allow England to focus all its energies on defeating Hitler—was broken in February 1944, once Germany's defeat seemed inevitable. In the ten months prior to Joshua and Isadora's arrival in Palestine, the Irgun had bombed British government and security offices in Jerusalem, Tel Aviv, and Haifa. British policemen and soldiers had been shot, railway lines mined, and critical military infrastructure sabotaged. A full-scale revolt had begun. The British responded with perpetual manhunts for Irgun fighters, and the punishment for any Jew caught with an illegal weapon was life in prison or death by hanging.

"Sure it was risky," my grandfather told me. "You always had to be on guard, and never knew who you could trust, so you couldn't trust anyone but a few close contacts. Especially since some Jews were better friends to the British than they were to us."

For years, the Irgun and its Jewish Agency–led counterpart, the Haganah, had worked toward similar goals, but with vastly different philosophies. During the late 1930s, when waves of Arab attacks terrorized the Yishuv, the Haganah, as ordered by Ben-Gurion, followed a policy of restraint: On one hand, its leaders felt bound to take the moral high road, not wanting to become terrorists themselves; on the other, they were cautious of sparking an endless blood feud with the people they knew they'd be living side by side with for years to come. The Irgun, believing that strength, and the willingness to exercise it, was the only deterrent the Arabs would respect—and that restraint would be interpreted as cowardice—made good on its promise to take one Arab life for every settler who was killed. While many in the Yishuv admired their daring, even ruthless, retaliations against the Arabs, the Jewish Agency considered them a bunch of lawless, radical thugs. In the 1940s, the Agency adopted a conciliatory stance toward the British, believing it'd ultimately be advantageous to stay on their good side. As the Irgun hit target after British target, the Agency felt the Irgun was damaging the Jewish cause. The Haganah began feeding intelligence about the Irgun to the British army, and even helped capture their fellow countrymen, handing over upward of one thousand of them (about half of their force). In a few instances, the Haganah tortured Irgun fighters, squeezing them for information about their operations.

Irgun members were outraged. If the British or the Arabs had done to them what the Haganah was doing, they'd have avenged themselves with force. Many in the Irgun agitated to retaliate. Their own had become their enemy. The Yishuv sped toward the brink of a violent implosion. But Menachem Begin slammed on the brakes, declaring that there would be no civil war. Facing down many of his angry followers, he ordered them not to strike the Haganah. With an ethic of discipline deeply sown among the ranks, Begin's fighters obeyed. Full-scale disaster was averted, but tensions and suspicions remained. The Haganah continued to collaborate with the British, who continued to hunt the Irgun.

In an orange grove near the insane asylum, Joshua and three other new recruits were taught to clean, load, and fire pistols and machine guns, though they didn't do too much shooting, not wanting to waste ammunition or attract attention. They practiced wiring and planting explosives, but only blew things up on occasional field trips into the desert. Joshua, recalling the training he'd received with his Betar youth group back in Uzhgorod, quickly mastered these skills. He soon became a weapons instructor himself, and hid firearms in dirty sheets under his and Isadora's bed in the mental hospital without her knowing it.

THIRTY-SIX

My grandfather, the terrorist. The stuff of family legend.

The stories never get tired of being told, with some kind of disagreement over one minor detail or another: "That happened before Gary was born"; "No, it had to be after"; "No, I really think it was before"—followed by the fumbling creation of a verbal timeline to conclusively determine whether or not the episode in question occurred before or after my father came into the world.

There was the time my grandfather went to the orange grove to train a couple of new Irgun fighters. He wended his way among the fruit-laden trees, a machine gun in a sack that he carried under his arm. He arrived at the meeting place, stood with his back against a tree, and waited. About ten minutes after the appointed time, he heard footsteps. He'd have to teach these guys something about punctuality, he thought, as he emerged from the shade and went to meet them. But instead of young revolutionary recruits, he found himself heading straight toward a team of British soldiers. They wore tennis shoes, so the story goes, so they could sneak around the orchard, quietly hunting for insurgents. If they had caught him with the gun, he'd surely have gone to jail—if he wasn't shot on the spot.

Joshua made a split-second decision. Neither faltering nor quickening his pace, he strode confidently toward the patrol. "If I had tried to run away," my grandfather said, "they would have chased me until they caught or killed me." His only chance was to bet that the soldiers would make the reasonable assumption that anyone who was unafraid to approach them couldn't be doing anything wrong. He greeted them courteously, then passed right by them, unmolested. As soon as he turned a corner and knew he was out of sight, his composure fled, and he sprinted away toward the asylum. At the orchard's edge, he was met by a friend who had come to give him a message, but had taken cover when he'd seen the soldiers heading directly toward where Joshua was supposed to be. "He nearly fainted when he saw me," my grandfather recalled with satisfied grin. "He was sure I was dead."

He had an even closer call about a year later, the story of which is my grandmother's favorite, since she plays a crucial role. By the time it took place, her life had changed significantly. She and Joshua had come to know each other well and had truly fallen in love. While Joshua was busy working wood and doing his part to fight the British, Isadora had found work as a maternity nurse at Hadassah Hospital in Tel Aviv, through a friend of Bela's who happened to be the janitor of the ward. There, she learned to speak Hebrew, and realized that in her new language, her nickname, *Isa*, sounded like the word for "goat." She took a new name, calling herself Aviva, like Joshua's sister—which, I'm told, was not considered unusual during that time. She'd also become pregnant. Despite helping deliver countless babies and being on familiar terms with the doctors, she avoided seeing one for nearly her entire pregnancy, embarrassed about being seen naked by a man. Finally, during her eighth month, the other nurses, who felt like older sisters to Isadora, swore they'd strip her themselves and drag her to the obstetrician if she refused to go for a checkup. She went.

Not long after she was declared healthy, my grandparents were at their rented house in a newly built community in Givat Shmuel. Joshua was on the couch, reading the paper, and Isadora was preparing for bed when her water suddenly broke, soaking her nightgown. They looked at each other in panic; Joshua had no idea what had happened, and was sure the baby was going to burst out onto the floor any second. The man who had so coolly deceived a group of British soldiers was so unnerved that he literally started eating the newspaper he was holding. One thought alone filled his head: He had to call the ambulance. But it was eleven o'clock on a pitch-black night. The nearest phone belonged to a neighbor who lived about two hundred yards away and whose orchard was patrolled by two huge hounds.

As Joshua opened the gate and dashed down the walkway, the dogs leapt out from the trees behind him and gave chase, barking terrifying threats. He made it to the safety of the front porch, slamming the door behind him just as one of the dogs lunged for his leg. After phoning for an ambulance, he returned home and noticed he'd cut a finger somewhere along the way; he was so worked up that he bandaged the wrong one, and didn't realize it until hours later. Their first child, named Gidon (which he changed to Gary once the family moved to America), was born in the early hours of the morning, on December 12, 1945. For Joshua and Isadora, there was profound joy. It wasn't simply the overwhelming emotion that normally accompanies a new child, one's own child, into the world.

Earlier that year, not long after the war in Europe had ended, Joshua had learned the fates of his mother and sister in Auschwitz, and heard that his father hadn't made it out of Mauthausen alive, though it would be many more years before he discovered exactly how Bela was killed. To Joshua, this made the birth of his first son even more momentous: His family would live on. "In the big picture, your father was immediate, living proof that Hitler didn't succeed," my grandfather told me. Plus, having a baby gave him a perfect new place to hide weapons. My father's first nights were spent sleeping in a crib that doubled as an arms cache, with unloaded pistols tucked beneath his mattress. Parts of disassembled machine guns were stashed among the stacks of his clean cloth diapers. Joshua also kept a mimeograph machine hidden beneath a pile of rags in a closet, on which he duplicated flyers for the Irgun. By this time, Isadora knew what he was up to, and at first, she didn't like it. Joshua, using simple Hebrew words so she'd understand, had to convince her that he wasn't a terrorist, but a freedom fighter. He finally overcame her skepticism and won her support, despite her fears of his being caught.

Sometime in the spring or summer of 1946, Joshua became involved in a plot to hijack a British army truck that was carrying a load of dynamite. His role was to meet the hijackers at a designated place after they'd stolen the truck, then guide them to the secret storage facility. The Irgun didn't want the hijackers to know its whereabouts beforehand, in the event that they were captured and tortured by the British. Joshua took Isadora along with him, in order to look less conspicuous, and they waited under a tree like lovers on a date. Hours passed and no one showed up, so eventually they went home. Just after midnight, they were awoken by a knock at the door. It was an Irgun agent, who came to tell Joshua that the mission had gone bad. The soldier who was on the truck guarding the explosives had fired on the hijackers; they shot back, and killed him. They successfully commandeered the truck, left the driver unharmed along with the dead soldier, then sped off across the desert. But the truck got stuck in the sand just outside Givat Shmuel. The dynamite was unloaded and buried nearby, the truck was abandoned, and the Irgunists fled.

At six o'clock that morning, Joshua and Isadora were wakened again, this time by the sound of loudspeakers blaring in the street. All of the neighborhood's residents were ordered by the British army to get dressed and come outside within five minutes. They had searched all night for the dynamite, hadn't found it, and assumed it had been transferred to a nearby house. They intended to search each and every one until it turned up. Hundreds of soldiers surrounded the community, armed and ready for a fight. The women were told to stand outside their homes; the men were separated from them and marched to the end of the street to show their identity papers. One by one, the houses were searched. Joshua and Isadora's was the last on the block. She waited by the front steps, her nightgown covered by a robe, holding her infant son. There was no way that the soldiers, if they did a half-thorough job, could fail to discover the guns hidden in their home. Isadora struggled to appear calm while her mind was filled with visions of prison, having her child taken away from her, and facing the hangman.

At last, there was only one house left. The search team marched toward it. When the commanding officer reached the steps, he looked at Isadora, paused, then told his men to forget it—that searching this house would be a waste of time. They turned around and left. When I asked my grandmother why she thought they didn't go in, she said, "I really don't know. I guess because I was standing there, cradling this beautiful baby in the beautiful morning light, and they probably thought I looked like the Virgin Mary or something. Would the Virgin Mary be a terrorist?"

Like most in the Irgun, Joshua lived a double life. None of his neighbors knew he was in the underground; to them, he was just an average, law-abiding citizen whose main concerns were his family and his business. But even his business was an exercise in duplicity, serving as a front for the Irgun's illegal printing operations, which the British strove to eradicate; even teenage boys caught pasting newsletters on shop windows in Tel Aviv were arrested and imprisoned.

Joshua had agreed to set up a shop in a storefront rented by the Irgun in an Arab neighborhood in Jaffa, just outside of Tel Aviv. Before moving in his new woodworking equipment, which the Irgun had purchased for him as part of their plan, agents began to dig out a secret room under the floor. Accessible by a trap door, this basement would house a professional printing press. The racket made by Joshua's tools would cover the noise of the press, and air vents for the printing room could be connected to those from the woodshop without being too conspicuous. Besides, the Irgunists felt that Joshua's familiarity with printing equipment might come in handy in a pinch.

A few days into the excavation of the basement, the landlord, who was an Arab, came to Joshua and told him that two neighbors had seen a truck leave from behind the building, carrying away a load of dirt. There was only one place whence the dirt could have come and, though he didn't know exactly what it'd be used for, he knew that an underground room was being built. In a conspiratorial tone, the landlord said to my grandfather, "Listen—we're both fighting for the same thing. You want the British out so you can have your Jewish state here. I want the British out, so Transjordan will get its independence. If you help us, we'll help you. What do you think?"

Joshua played stupid, saying he had no idea what the landlord was talking about; then he reported the encounter to his handlers. Deemed too risky to stay at that location, it was abandoned for another, also in Jaffa, but bigger, and with a walled-in courtyard. This time, the printing press would be set up in a small room off of the main workshop, the door of which was completely concealed behind large wooden crates. Woodworking machinery was installed, and Joshua began filling orders for furniture and toys, with rocking horses becoming his specialty. But before the press was put into place, the workshop and the hidden room would be put to other, even more sensitive, purposes.

On June 13, 1946, two Irgun fighters who had been captured a few months earlier, during an attack on a British army base, were tried, found guilty, and sentenced to death. The British were in no mood for leniency, intending to use the men as examples. The Irgun concluded that the only way to save them was with a prisoner exchange. But first, they had to take prisoners. In preparation for the operation, Joshua, in his new workshop, built two large wooden boxes, each of which would fit perfectly in the back of a small truck and could be locked from the outside. On June 18, the two trucks were driven to downtown Tel Aviv and parked outside the British Officers' Club. An Irgun strike team wielding pistols and pipes raided the club and managed to abduct five of the officers who'd been having lunch. They were muscled out to the trucks, two loaded in one box, three in the other, and taken to separate locations. The truck with three hostages pulled up outside Joshua's shop, and the box was hefted by a team of men into the hidden room that was the intended home of the printing press.

The British imposed a round-the-clock curfew on Tel Aviv. Armed search parties cordoned off and scoured the neighborhoods, looking for the servicemen. The city's squares and major intersections were surrounded by machine-gun batteries, and roads leading out of town were sealed. By this time, the Jewish Agency had stopped hunting the Irgun and had even given the go-ahead for the Haganah to engage in joint operations with the Revisionist militia— a change brought about by broken British promises to open immigration in 1945. But the Agency's leadership had no idea that the Irgun planned to kidnap British soldiers, and publicly denounced the action as "insane." Afraid of likely repercussions, Ben-Gurion pressed the Irgun to release them. The day following the abductions, however, the Irgun seized another British officer, who managed to escape his captors the following afternoon. Yet, despite the many thousands of man-hours spent hunting for them, the whereabouts of the original five hostages remained unknown.

After a few days, the Irgun freed the two hostages that weren't being held at the woodshop. One was given a clean shirt, both were given one-pound notes to compensate them for "wear and tear." Their eyes were covered with opaque goggles, and they were driven to a corner near the Officers' Club where they'd been kidnapped. Before being released, the soldiers were given a message to pass on to their superiors: If the British executed the two Irgun fighters recently sentenced to death, the still-missing officers would be killed, too.

With the situation completely out of their control, the British intensified their sweep. On June 29, over a thousand Jews were arrested, including four top Jewish Agency officials. Three Jews were killed, a handful injured, and a curfew was placed over the entirety of the Yishuv. Within three days, over 2,700 Jews had been rounded up and sent to detention camps.

Meanwhile, three British officers remained bound in the secret room in my grandfather's shop. They were guarded but not gagged or blindfolded, and were treated respectfully, receiving two good meals each day, plus afternoon tea. As the days elapsed, a surprisingly friendly rapport developed between the hostages and their captors. Wearing a mask over his face, Joshua would visit with them from time to time. The officers understood why they'd been abducted, and seemed to sympathize with the Zionist cause. One of them, Joshua learned, had served in India, and had guarded Gandhi when he'd been in British custody. A few thousand Jews, the officer joked, were causing as much trouble for the Empire as were a few hundred million Indians.

Two weeks after the kidnappings, with no hope of finding the officers, the Mandatory High Commissioner commuted the sentence of the two Irgun fighters to life in prison. The following day, the hostages were crammed back into the box, which was hoisted onto the bed of a truck and driven to downtown Tel Aviv. On Rothschild Boulevard, the box was lowered into the street. The three dazed officers stumbled out as the truck sped away.

The operation went exactly as planned, except for one slipup: The Irgun agents who had come to retrieve the officers were dressed in suits and ties. They didn't appear anything like the kind of people who'd be expected to be moving and lifting industrial-sized crates out of a wood shop. While they were loading up, Joshua noticed that an Arab grocer had been watching them from across the street. All of the newspapers were filled with accounts of the hostage release—including descriptions of the box they'd been left in. "It bothered me that night. I had a feeling he was going to put two and two together," my grandfather said of the grocer. The next day, he approached his shop with unusual caution; as he came within eyeshot, he saw the place being ransacked by soldiers. He turned around, walked away, and never went back.

Soon, another building was secured for the printing press, this time in a Jewish neighborhood in Tel Aviv. New woodworking machinery was purchased, and Joshua began making sofa frames there for an American company whose owner supported the underground. The press was installed in a room excavated beneath the tiled floor, accessed through a trapdoor in the corner. Ink and newsprint was smuggled in among the raw lumber, and the workshop became the new publishing house for the Irgun's newspaper, called *Herut*. Written almost entirely by Menachem Begin, who lived in hiding, it was among his most powerful mediums for getting his message directly to the people of the Yishuv. Despite the dangers of printing and distributing it, *Herut* was produced continuously until Israel achieved independence.

———————

The Irgun continued to resist against the British, convinced they wouldn't voluntarily abdicate their colonial mandate. Hardly a week went by without multiple incidents, with scores of British soldiers and policemen killed in ambushes, targeted assassinations, and attacks on military installations. Though the British military presence surged from 80,000 to 100,000 troops, they were unable to reign in fewer than 2,000 Irgunists. The security situation descended into complete chaos, and by the end of 1946, British soldiers retreated into heavily fortified "green zones" when not on patrol, imprisoning themselves for their own survival.

In addition to the everyday acts of sabotage and violence, the Irgun executed a number of high-profile assaults for maximum international visibility. On July 22, 1946, they blew up the headquarters of the British Secretariat, located in Jerusalem's King David Hotel; a telephoned warning to the hotel went unheeded, and ninety-one people died as the entire southwestern wing of the six-story building collapsed. The Irgun took their war to European soil on October 31, bombing the British Embassy in Rome; soon, wild rumors swept through England of an imminent (though never, in fact, planned) Irgun attack on London itself. In Palestine, British soldiers were seized and publicly lashed; a popular officers' club in the supposedly impenetrable green zone was destroyed on a Saturday night; and on May 4, 1947, Acre Prison—an old Crusader fortress that had once repelled the forces of Napoleon, and was used by the British to jail, and hang, members of the Jewish resistance—became the target of what newspapers around the world called "the greatest jailbreak in history." Two months later, two British sergeants were kidnapped, then hung, in retaliation for the executions of three Irgun fighters. No strong-arm attempt to smother the Jewish revolt achieved even the slightest degree of success.

Some British newspapers called for an all-out assault on the Yishuv, but soon, as Irgun attacks continued unabated, and as the British national reputation was smeared due to the inhuman treatment of the Jewish refugees aboard the ship *Exodus*, public taste for maintaining the Mandate soured beyond recovery.

Throughout this time, my grandfather continued to train Irgun fighters, to store weapons, and to act as a front for their publishing operations. He was, I believe, rarely, if ever, included in direct attacks on British forces. I say "I believe" because of one story I was told, shortly before his death in 2007, long after I thought I had heard all about his involvement during the revolt.

The Irgun had determined that there was a spy among their ranks, selling intelligence to the British. He was a Polish Jew who, upon investigation, was discovered to have once been a Nazi collaborator back in Europe, trading information about his brethren in exchange for his own safety. The Germans had permitted him to escape to Palestine, where he embedded himself in the underground as a British secret agent. Moles in the Irgun were a rarity, and that was the way it had to stay. Joshua and two of his comrades were summoned by the leadership, and given orders handed down directly by Begin.

They arranged to meet the traitor one balmy summer night at a park in Tel Aviv, under false pretenses. When they arrived, their unsuspecting target was sitting calmly on a bench, under a tree. My grandfather and the other two Irgunists surrounded the spy, pulled pistols from their pants, and aimed them at his head. There was no chance of escape. They grilled him, needing to confirm for their own consciences that the accusations were true. Terrified for his life, the spy confessed, both to collaborating with the British and to his complicity with the Nazis, providing details too specific to be invented. He begged for mercy, hyperventilating, with tears streaming from his eyes.

Now that the moment had come, any righteous anger that had risen in the hearts of the interrogators vanished, so upset were they at the prospect of killing another Jew. The appointed assassin, who stood to the right of my grandfather, hesitated. Then he fired once. His hand was shaking so badly when he pulled the trigger that the bullet failed to instantly kill the spy. Having spent all of his nerves on the first shot, he didn't deliver a second. My grandfather and the other two hit men fled. The spy, critically injured, was discovered by passersby and taken to the hospital, where he died.

When my grandfather told me this story, he did so matter-of-factly, with no self-glorification, but also no shame. It was an act committed against an enemy during wartime. And that was how I accepted it. But I was left to wonder, since I'd learned of this incident so late in his life, if there were other stories he'd kept to himself.

THIRTY-SEVEN

I traveled by bus to the Romanian port of Constanta, hoping to find passage on a ship sailing for Istanbul, so I could see, more or less, where it was that my grandparents met. Unfortunately, the ferryboat that sails between the two cities during the summer months was already docked for the winter.

I wandered around the shipyard, meandering along jetties, marveling at the rows of towering yellow cranes that were poised like the arms of gigantic praying mantises. A blustery drear hung over the coast, with drizzle flung sideways by gusts driven across the water. The surface of the sea was roiled with whitecaps, making it appear a shade or two lighter than its name implies. I stopped by the offices of a few commercial shipping companies, asking if there was a cargo boat leaving for Istanbul that I could hop aboard. The most favorable answer was, "Maybe in a week, maybe in two." My grandparents had an easier time getting a ship out of Constanta than I was having, so I took the bus to Istanbul instead.

After a few days of roaming the streets and bazaars of what is surely one of the world's great cities, I headed south, to the stretch of land between Konya and Adana, somewhere along which Joshua and Isadora were married. A blizzard struck during my journey, burying the fields and pastures beneath inches of snow, turning the undulating hills that rippled the steppes into gleaming white dunes, as it had looked when my grandparents were wed. Naturally, I reflected on the events that had brought them together, still astounded that they ever happened to meet. Of all possible fates, the crossing of their paths, paved with countless cobblestones laid by chance, was so unlikely it seemed miraculous.

Ingesting their story as a child had infused me with the conviction that all terrible events are necessary chapters of a larger story which ultimately has a happy ending; that, in a sense, human history is riding along a fundamentally benevolent teleological track, propelled, in part, by tragedy. These ideas held me for many years, and gave me a sense of trust in the workings of the world despite its chronic bouts of cruelty. Eventually, however, I came to see these beliefs as wistful rationalizations invented by a child's mind, which allowed him to make sense of his existence; I'd been like a young Pangloss who had to believe that this is the best of all possible worlds in order to swallow its myriad of horrors, including those that produced him. As I grew older, I saw too much meanness on the planet, too many innocents perpetually suffering at the hands of men, for such a sunny scenario to remain plausible.

Of course, sunshine follows rain, April showers bring May flowers, and one can profit from loss. One of the spiritual teachings of Judaism is that "ascent follows descent," and that our descents have meaning, in part because they stimulate the next ascent. It's very tempting to think of tragedy as having the motive of bringing about the positive things that emerge from it. But to grant tragedy the dignity of having intention is to say that everything happens for a reason, and for the life of me, I can no longer imagine any reason that is worth genocide, war, and oppression. I can't explain them away as crucial, if disturbing, catalysts of a positive human trajectory, since there is nothing inherent in the logos of history that guarantees the human condition will improve; that's up to us. And since none of the particular events for which we are grateful are pre-ordained, none of the particular sufferings that helped produce them actually had to happen. They are, simply, not necessary.

As my faith in human events being guided by an intelligent hand eroded over the years, as my notion of God faded into arche-typal abstraction, I fell victim to a case of philosophical whiplash that produced a malignant agnosticism. For a time, I began to think that maybe I'd become something along the lines of a progressive nihilist: convinced that life had no meaning, but that we are bound by moral imperatives nonetheless; that even though everything is pointless, human beings are obliged to treat each other well.

I'd like to say that I had a revelation on the road to Adana, a personal Paulian moment that lifted me from the existential abyss. It didn't quite happen like that. But over the course of my immersion in the landscape of my own creation myth, questions of ultimate mean-ing came to matter less. I became captivated instead by the mystery that swirls through life, looking with newfound awe at the incredible stories that unfold as if they were scripted, at those moments pro-found and surprising enough to persuade even a skeptic into allowing that something more might be going on here than meets the eye.

Despite an awareness that this is not the best of all possible worlds, I'm struck time and again by an elusive sense of perfection, like a phenomenon you can only glimpse with your peripheral vision, which disappears when you turn to view it head-on. It's a perfection replete with contradiction: ideals and hypocrisies, synchronicity and randomness, kindness and cruelty, love and fear, splendor and squa-lor, grace and catastrophe, things that are and dreams of what might have been—all of which, when simmered together, tastes like Truth. And at these times, it seems like Keats was onto something when he wrote that "Truth is beauty," as ugly as it sometimes is.

Aside from the pure wonder of experiencing those moments, I also wonder about them. I don't know whether truth *is* beauty and I happen to glimpse it every so often, or if I have the luxury of deceiving myself on occasion, because it helps, and because I haven't been broken enough by the world to *really* know that some things could never be a part of anything beautiful. I don't know if it's possible to integrate the beauty of the ugliness without diminishing the ugliness of ugliness; if attempting to do so is a spiritual act or one of denial. Did Onu Weissglass, writing inspirational poetry in Transnistria, perceive something real that others didn't, and that sustained him, or was he escaping into a fabrication that helped him tolerate epic misery and unmitigated insanity?

At the moment, I'm content with having no answers to these questions, with swimming around in them for a while and being able to truly wonder. The only thing I derive with certainty from contemplating my grandparents' lives is that it's our collective task to diminish, as much as humanly possible, the ugliness for which we are responsible.

I'd intended to continue on to Israel, which I'd previously visited a number of times, but for various reasons didn't get there on this trip. The closest I came was the Turkish town of Harran, just north of the Syrian border. The Bible notes that Abraham and Sarah settled temporarily in Harran on their way from Ur to the land of Canaan, and that it was the home of Laban, the brother of Rebecca and father-in-law (and uncle) of Jacob. It's among the most ancient inhabited towns on earth, famous for its beehive-shaped adobe houses that stay cool in summer and warm in winter, most of which have been abandoned for the luxury of modern cinder-block rectangles.

I was traveling for the moment with a friend of a friend who lived in Istanbul, named Merve, who had curly blonde locks that cascaded over her shoulders, a sweet smile, and a charming way of articulating the delicate staccato patter of the Turkish language. She always had a scarf coiled around her neck, and wore jeans rolled up just above the tops of her polka-dotted rubber boots.

The houses of Harran were spread among ruins of collapsed mud-brick buildings, and some of the ruins themselves served as homes. Kids played among them, smudged with poverty yet animated by youth, little sparks of life floating brightly amid dusty destitution. Emaciated horses stood sullenly in yards scattered with trash, over which bedsheets hanging out to dry billowed in the breeze. The smoky skyline was transected by power lines strung between metal latticework towers.

We came to a small museum, a perfectly restored traditional home, with eleven beehive rooms laid out in an L along two sides of a spacious walled courtyard. It took only minutes to appreciate the exhibit, but we were in no hurry. The docents, guards, and curators of the museum were the three children who called it home; there were no adults around. The eldest was an eleven-year-old boy who wore a dark pinstriped suit jacket over a plaid shirt, and had the kind of face that made it easy to imagine what he'd look like in old age. His sister, who was nine, was modestly dressed in an ankle-length black-and-white-checked skirt, a maroon sweater, and an impeccably arranged headscarf tied under her chin, framing her softly featured face and concealing every single strand of her hair. The youngest was seven, a boy in a zippered sweater who closely resembled his brother, but for his noticeably larger ears. Like most of the town's residents, they were ethnic Arabs, but spoke Turkish.

With Merve interpreting, we talked to them for a few minutes about their house, and they showed us how they drew water from a well in the courtyard. Then we sat on low stools around a table made from an old millstone, and played game after game of mankala, in which pebbles are moved around a cupped wooden board. The girl played thoughtfully, planning her moves a few steps ahead; her older brother played with a prescience that allowed him to move his stones with instinctual speed; not having played in about twenty years, I shuttled my pieces recklessly, not caring much if I lost. It was a pleasure simply to play and laugh with them.

In the midst of a game, two mustachioed Turkish men strode into the courtyard. They were tourists who'd come to see the ancient city. After a few words of greeting, they sized up the situation, and gruffly asked Merve, who was sitting beside me, what she was doing with a foreigner, implying that such a thing was degrading to her Turkish honor.

Before she could formulate a response, and as instinctually as he moved his mankala pieces, the eleven-year-old spoke up.

"Because he's human and she's human," he said.

The men repeated their question, with an edge of menace, and the boy, perfectly composed, faced them down. "You have no right to ask her that," he said. "You need to leave."

The men's bravado flagged and they slunk away, defeated by a young boy's assertion of a simple truth that, sadly, felt profound. ⊂━━×⊱

THIRTY-EIGHT

Beginning on November 29, 1947, with the United Nations partition of Palestine into Jewish and Arab states, and followed by the declaration of Israeli independence on May 14, 1948, the next few years of my grandparents' lives—and those of all Israelis—were dominated by war with the Arabs. In the months prior to independence, before there was a unified Israeli army, Joshua fought with the Irgun against the local Arab militias, while foreign Arab armies waited on the sidelines for the British to evacuate. In his old Hillman car, with its round headlights looking like wide-open eyes and fenders that swooped back over the wheel wells to form running boards, Joshua raced into combat like motorized cavalry, with a machine gunner firing away through the sunroof. After independence—when the newborn nation of Israel merged its various militias into a single army to defend against simultaneous attacks by Egypt, Jordan, Syria, Iraq, and Lebanon—Joshua was inducted as a staff sergeant.

Over the next fourteen months, he'd rise to the rank of captain, serving as staff officer in charge of supplies for elite commando units fighting in the Negev. He became the right-hand man to Chaim Bar-Lev, who would later serve as Israel's defense minister, and was on the scene when Beersheba, Ein Gedi, and Eilat fell into Israeli hands. Joshua's position usually allowed him to spend one night a week at home, for Shabbat.

Meanwhile, Isadora remained at their new house in Ramat Gan, along with her brother, Yisrael, who'd moved in after Isa pleaded with him not to join the army. She had lost all of her close family but him, and couldn't bear the thought of him being killed in combat, however noble the cause. Once he was persuaded, Joshua spoke with some of his personal connections and secured Yisrael a military deferment.

Isadora quit work to be a full-time mother and hostess to a revolving crowd of aunts, uncles, and cousins who emigrated from Romania soon after Israeli independence had been declared. They stayed with Isa and Yisrael for weeks or months at a time, however long it took them to get settled on their own. As soon as two left, three more would arrive. It was then that she got the news: Her uncles, Sami and Dutsu, who had vanished one night into the Transnistrian countryside, had made it safely into Soviet territory and had survived the war. And her aunt Mitzi, who she'd long ago given up for dead, wasn't; she and the priest who had helped them in Obodovka were imprisoned for years in the city of Balta, but for some unknown reason, they weren't killed. Mitzi was back in Bucharest, teaching French. Isadora melted with joy. Nothing she'd ever heard had made her as happy.

She welcomed any relative who came, even those who had been unwilling to help them when she and Yisrael had returned to Bucharest as orphans. She would have even let her uncle Herman— the one who owned the clothing store—stay with her, if Joshua hadn't put his foot down. The others, he'd rationalized, hadn't been in much of a position to help Isadora back then, but there were no excuses for a man with a large apartment and a thriving business to abandon his niece and nephew to an orphanage. Joshua wouldn't let him in the house, even for a minute—but perhaps he should have thanked Herman instead; if he'd have opened his home to Isadora and Yisrael in Bucharest, they would never have set foot on the *Toros*.

The overcrowded house in Ramat Gan, filled with the sound of Romanian voices, was comforting in its familiarity. Isadora had grown up and lived her whole life, until the war, in homes with more people than beds. Only now, rather than simply struggling to survive with little hope of ever really prospering, the mood in the house was bright with possibilities. With Joshua away so often, she was glad to have the company and help with raising her young son. My father's first spoken words were in the Romanian in which he was immersed.

My father has a few clear memories from his earliest years: the plaintive wail of air-raid sirens, followed by a mad scramble to the middle of the house, which was said to be the safest place to be; his father returning home from the army on Friday afternoons and shooting the heads off of live chickens, which Isadora would pluck and cook for dinner; and a single shriek, so earsplitting, so anguished, it seared itself forever in his brain, when his mother lifted his three-month-old sister out of the carriage after an hour-long walk to find that she was dead.

Soon after the War of Independence ended, Joshua and Isadora, following a patriotic trend encouraged among immigrants, changed their European surname to Hebrew. They chose Ben-Anav, *Ben* meaning "son of," and *Anav* being a direct translation of *Szereny*, meaning "humble." Bela himself had occasionally signed his essays "Anav," to express his sense of Jewish nationalism. Following their move to the

United States a few years later, the name was condensed to what it is today. For me, the name is loaded with everything that contributed to its evolution—from the global to the personal; from vast cruelties to minor miracles.

———

The family was lured to America by a business opportunity my grandfather couldn't refuse. The move was meant to be temporary, a few years at most. But aside from the economic incentives to stay, Isadora, with four sons by the end of the 1950s, couldn't contemplate sending her children into the Israeli army and possibly losing another one. And Joshua, despite feeling that Israel was where he and his family belonged, couldn't bring himself to pressure his wife to return. With hard work, ingenuity, and an awful head for business, he built for them a comfortable, middle-class suburban life, and the children thrived; nevertheless, Joshua always felt a pinch of regret that they weren't living in the country that he and his father had devoted so much to creating. Late in life, he felt at times that he'd made a terrible mistake by remaining in America, especially after his three oldest grandchildren chose to marry outside of the tribe. My grandmother was less judgmental about intermarriage, happy, simply, that we had found good people to love.

———

The Holocaust convinced both Joshua and Isadora of the impossibility of the existence of a God; something Joshua asserted with his typical confidence and Isadora said only quietly, just in case there actually was a God and He happened to be listening. Yet their atheism in no way diluted their sense of being Jewish. "It's very important for me to be Jewish, for my children and grandchildren to be Jewish," my grandfather said. "I've fought for it. My parents and my sister were killed for it. And 'Jewish' to me is more than a religion; I grew up in a milieu in which it was considered first and foremost a nationality, a history, a moral way of living. I can be a Jew very comfortably without believing in God."

In the way that I came to know them, my grandmother seemed less beholden to the past than my grandfather. She has an innate ability to integrate all of the good things in her life into her experience of the world, and wholeheartedly expresses the ecstatic jubilation or devastating grief of whatever celebration or tragedy is at hand. At a bar mitzvah or a wedding, no one would dance with more joyous abandon. When she would talk about the war years, which wasn't often, her emotions surged painfully to the surface, and she'd be momentarily overcome by loss. She has no explanation for how or why she survived the forced marches, the typhus epidemic, the frozen hell that was Transnistria. "Maybe it was fate," she told me. "Some people say it must have been a will to survive—but what will to survive? I was so sick and hungry that I had no will, and it didn't seem like there was anything worth surviving for anyway."

Joshua, while never a bitter man and truly an optimist at heart, seemed perpetually connected by an invisible umbilicus to his roots and to what the Nazis had done to his family. Though rarely dour— he loved to laugh, and make others laugh—there was a part of him that was never perfectly at peace. The loss of his family was accepted as fact, but never truly reconciled. He employed cognitive coping mechanisms, becoming an amateur (and encyclopedic) Holocaust expert and Jewish history scholar, immensely proud of the vast accomplishments of his people yet ever mindful of their vulnerability. He remained vigilant against the forces that sought to wipe Jews from the face of the earth—especially the Arabs—and believed the only security that Jews could possibly have in this world was that which they created by their own strength. When asked once what life-lesson he'd like to convey to future generations, he answered, "Don't trust in the future, and never bury your head in the sand."

Remembering was as close to a sacred duty as he could conceive. Every Passover, as the family sat around the Seder table laden with the ritual foods of redemption, he'd read passages from the last letter he received from his parents; partly so they wouldn't be forgotten, and partly, I think, to help us all appreciate what it means to be free. He read with a touch of sadness, but mostly with low simmering outrage, as though issuing a quiet call to arms against anyone who might try to persecute our people again.

———•••••———

In the late 1960s, Joshua received a letter from a friend of his father's, by the name of Izso Schonbrunn, who had lived in Uzhgorod and, like Bela, had been deported to Auschwitz, then transferred to Mauthausen. This was the only "grade III" complex in the entire concentration camp system—a ranking distinguishing it as the cruelest of all labor camps, designed to work every last inmate to death. Though there were gas chambers, the most notorious feature of Mauthausen was its stone quarry, where prisoners hacked granite blocks from the walls of a narrow chasm, which they were then forced to carry on their backs, up 186 steep and uneven steps. So many fell as they climbed that the steps became known as the Stairway of Death. More deportees perished at Mauthausen than at any other labor camp (in contrast to more blatantly dubbed "extermination camps"), most murdered with work, disease, and malnutrition, but many thousands also gassed, shot, and beaten to death.

Schonbrunn had been a tailor before being deported, and was initially assigned to patch clothing and blankets for the guards. Needing extra help, he obtained permission for Bela to work as his partner, rescuing him from the lethal labor of the stone quarry where he first toiled. Schonbrunn taught Bela how to sew, and soon they ingratiated themselves to the camp doctors by offering to repair their uniforms and stitch new collars onto their shirts. In exchange, the doctors saw to it that their tailors got double portions of food and were spared from the barbarous medical experiments performed on prisoners. "Every Friday night," Schonbrunn wrote to Joshua, "there was a lineup where they selected the ones to be gassed that week. When they came to me and your father, the doctors intervened, saying, 'These two are doing work for us,' and we were saved each time.

"Your father commemorated his wedding anniversary with a poem he wrote with tears in his eyes. He was also writing a book, which he hoped to save until the war was over; I was able to obtain paper and pencils for him. We always hoped that we would survive. There were maybe 12,000 prisoners in Mauthausen and the meager food was hardly enough for that many. When the American and Russian troops closed in, another 30,000 prisoners were brought to the camp, and there was no more food. Posters appeared, saying that those that wished to survive should volunteer to work at the factories surrounding the camp, and there they'd be supplied with food. Perhaps that's when I damaged my heart, when I looked around and saw that my friend, your father, was gone."

People all around them were dying of starvation. Corpses piled up around the barracks. Bela was persuaded by another friend to go where the food was, and he was transferred to the sub-camp, Ebensee, where he was put to work in a weapons factory. As the most valued laborers, they'd be the last to lose their rations. One day, a bread truck arrived, bringing loaves for the German and Austrian guards. A group of Jews was ordered to unload it, and Bela was among them. While carrying the bread into the mess hall, one of the prisoners stole a loaf. The guards saw it disappear, but didn't notice exactly who took it. They grabbed Bela, accused him of the theft, and pummeled him to death with the butts of their rifles. Bela never pointed out the real culprit, probably, according to an eyewitness, because he knew they'd just kill them both. He was murdered in April 1945—only a few weeks before the camp was liberated by American troops.

"I must say," Schonbrunn's letter read, "that your father, as if he had an intuition, remarked to me on one of the last times I saw him, 'My dear friend, if you live and get home, tell those of my family who survive this insanity that I always loved them very much.' " ❦

Index of Places

Acknowledgments

Many thanks are owed to my agent, Jennifer Joel, and my editors, Tom McCarthy, Ellen Urban, and especially Christine Duffy, whose enthusiasm for this project was inspirational. Thanks also to Vincent Slatt, librarian at the United States Holocaust Memorial Museum, for repeatedly directing me to sources essential to my historical research, and to Kate Clemans, Beth Goldman, and my uncle, Jay Benanav, for helping me find translators fluent in Hungarian and Hebrew. Stephen Dachi translated the story by Maxim Gorki, as well as one of the letters to my grandfather, written by Iszo Schonbrunn; Katharina Liston translated a number of articles and essays from *Zsido Neplap* and the *Jewish Family Almanac*; Ziva Moyal translated articles about the occupation of the mental asylum in B'nai Barak; my appreciation goes to each of them. Thanks to Arthur Gelb for his ever-wise counsel and to Howard Fishman, for companionship on part of my journey to Eastern Europe. Crucial parts of this book would have been missing without the many contributions of Renee Wexer, who spoke to me about her experiences during the war.

No part of this book would have been possible without the many hours, over a period of years, that my grandparents Joshua and Aviva (Isadora) Benanav spent telling me about their lives. Sadly, my grandfather died a few months before the book was completed. It would have been a dream come true for him to see it in print.

I'm infinitely grateful to Kelly Wolpert, whose oceans of understanding enabled me to write—and to sleep in after late nights of work—while she bore the lion's share of responsibility for tending to our newborn son, Lucas, whose first year of life coincided with the writing of this book. She is a miracle to me, and so is he.

About the Author

Michael Benanav is a prize-winning freelance writer and photographer, who seeks out compelling stories and images from remote regions around the world. His work has appeared in the New York Times, the International Herald Tribune, lonelyplanet.com, Hand/Eye, The Salt Journal, and other publications. His highly praised first book, Men of Salt: Crossing the Sahara on the Caravan of White Gold, for which he embarked on a 1,000-mile odyssey with one of the last working camel caravans on the planet, was nominated for Barnes & Noble's Discover Prize, and named a Best Book for Young Adults by the American Library Association. Also a veteran wilderness guide, he leads groups through the mountains and canyons of the American West. He lives in northern New Mexico.